Decolonising
Intervention

KILOMBO: INTERNATIONAL RELATIONS AND COLONIAL QUESTIONS

This is the first series to mark out a dedicated space for advanced critical inquiry into colonial questions across International Relations. The ethos of this book series is reflected by the bricolage constituency of Kilombos – settlements of African slaves, rebels and indigenous peoples in South America who became self-determining political communities that retrieved and renovated the social practices of its diverse constituencies while being confronted by colonial forces. The series embraces a multitude of methods and approaches, theoretical and empirical scholarship, alongside historical and contemporary concerns. Publishing innovative and top-quality peer-reviewed scholarship, Kilombo enquires into the shifting principles of colonial rule that inform global governance and investigates the contestation of these principles by diverse peoples across the globe. It critically re-interprets popular concepts, narratives and approaches in the field of IR by reference to the 'colonial question' and, in doing so, the book series opens up new vistas from which to address the key political questions of our time.

Series Editors:

Mustapha K. Pasha, Aberystwyth University
Meera Sabaratnam, SOAS University of London
Robbie Shilliam, Queen Mary University of London

Titles in the Series:

Meanings of Bandung: Postcolonial Orders and Decolonial Visions, Quỳnh N. Phạm and Robbie Shilliam
Politics of the African Anticolonial Archive, Shiera S. el-Malik and Isaac A. Kamola
Asylum after Empire: Colonial Legacies in the Politics of Asylum Seeking, Lucy Mayblin
Decolonising Intervention: International Statebuilding in Mozambique, Meera Sabaratnam
Unthinking the Colonial Myth of Complexity: Ethnocentrism, Hierarchy and the Global in International Relations, Gennaro Ascione (forthcoming)

Decolonising Intervention

International Statebuilding in Mozambique

Meera Sabaratnam

ROWMAN & LITTLEFIELD
INTERNATIONAL

London • New York

Published by Rowman & Littlefield International Ltd
Unit A, Whitacre Mews, 26–34 Stannary Street, London SE11 4AB
www.rowmaninternational.com

Rowman & Littlefield International Ltd.is an affiliate of Rowman & Littlefield
4501 Forbes Boulevard, Suite 200, Lanham, Maryland 20706, USA
With additional offices in Boulder, New York, Toronto (Canada), and Plymouth (UK)
www.rowman.com

British Library Cataloguing in Publication Data

A catalogue record for this book is available from the British Library

ISBN: HB 978-1-78348-274-0

Library of Congress Cataloging-in-Publication Data Available

ISBN: 978-1-78348-274-0 (cloth : alk. paper)
ISBN: 978-1-78348-275-7 (paperback)
ISBN: 978-1-78348-276-4 (electronic)

♾™ The paper used in this publication meets the minimum requirements of American
National Standard for Information Sciences—Permanence of Paper for Printed Library
Materials, ANSI/NISO Z39.48–1992.

Printed in the United States of America

*To the much-missed Dr. Sabapathy Sabaratnam
(1945–2013), who knew how to make a good case.*

Contents

Acknowledgements

This book project has cooked for a long time, and many have helped stir the pot. I warmly thank Celestino Jemusse Jackson Silva and Adélia Alberto Martíns for their research assistance in Mozambique. I thank them and Arcenia Guambe Horstmanshoff for their ongoing inspiration and friendship. I also express my deep gratitude towards all those interviewed across Mozambique who welcomed us, gave us their time and frank commentary on what was going on around them. I promised that you would remain unidentified in the project, but your generosity and insights made this project possible. Even though you told me what to put in this book, I hope it speaks back to you.

A number of very wonderful scholars have also generously supported this project through their feedback and commentary on the text and ideas. Special thanks go to Mark Hoffman, Kimberly Hutchings, Kirsten Ainley, Chris Alden and George Lawson for their input during its genesis as a doctoral project at the LSE, Chris Cramer for his comments on the thesis and Devon Curtis as I reworked the project at Cambridge. Joe Hanlon and Colin Darch helped me retrieve primary material relating to Mozambique at crucial junctures. Other important interlocutors for the project have included Tarak Barkawi, David Chandler, Julian Go, Lee Jones, Rahel Kunz, Suthaharan Nadarajah and David Rampton, plus the Bag of Dorks. I am particularly grateful for the feedback and input of Marta Iñiguez de Heredia, John Heathershaw, Kerem Nişancıoğlu and Rahul Rao on the draft chapters of the manuscript in its late stages. There are unpayable debts to Laleh Khalili, Robbie Shilliam and Mark Laffey for their generous, detailed and thoughtful comments on the entire manuscript. I would also like to express my gratitude to Anna Reeve, Dhara

Snowden and Mike Watson at Rowman & Littlefield International for their encouragement, accommodation and efficiency and to the reviewers for their guidance and feedback.

As always, love and thanks to my family for all their care and support and to Mark, who carried me over the line. This book is dedicated to my late father, who I think would have appreciated the argument.

Material support for the three research visits to Mozambique was provided by the Faculty of Law and Social Sciences at SOAS, University of London, the LSE Department of International Relations and the Economic and Social Research Council of the UK Government (ESRC ES/ F005431/1). Sections of the book and argument were also presented at the LSE International Theory Seminar, panels at the ISA on statebuilding and the liberal peace and a public lecture at Tecnológico de Monterrey, Mexico.

Chapter 2 is adapted from my article 'Avatars of Eurocentrism in the critique of liberal peace', published in *Security Dialogue*, Vol 44, No. 3 (2013), 259–78. The credit for the cartoon of *Xiconhoca*, figure 6.1, sourced from *Mozambique History Net*, is owed to Frelimo, Edição do Departamento de Trabalho Ideológico in Maputo and was likely published in the regular publication *Revista Tempo* around 1979. It has not been possible to secure copyright for the reproduction of this image so far, but the publishers will be pleased to address this in future editions of the work.

Chapter One

Introduction

I did not begin this study of post-war international statebuilding interventions expecting to find failure. I was in fact looking for success. Mozambique seemed worthy of study because of its relative neglect in the scholarly literature, except that it had been held up as a success story for peacebuilding and development. This was particularly in terms of the sequencing of its elections and demobilisation under UN auspices after the war ended in 1992. It had experienced high GDP growth, had held regular elections, had undertaken a series of economic and political restructuring measures with the support of international financial institutions, had a former president win the Mo Ibrahim Prize for African Leadership and recorded a marked drop in its level of absolute poverty between 1996–7 and 2003–4.[1] I read up on the theory and practice of peacebuilding and statebuilding, went through books on Mozambican history, processed the policy reports, looked at the profile of bilateral donors, multilateral agencies and NGOs in the country, learned Portuguese and set off.

Within three days of landing in the capital Maputo on a research visit in 2009, I went to a health sector capacity-building workshop in an upmarket hotel downtown to which I was warmly invited by the organiser. Community leaders from around the country were gathered by an international NGO to receive leadership training that would help them fight malaria. The American consultant running the workshop explained that one of the main problems with health systems in the developing world was not a lack of resources but the lack of leadership and management skills. However, the consultant was here to train attendees in 'The Challenge Model', which could then be used to help fight malaria. She promised that this would be one of the most practical classes they would ever take.

1

As the consultant did not speak Portuguese, the national administrative language in Mozambique, she spoke loudly and slowly in English, with a translator of variable quality summarising what she said. I looked around the room. The attendees were well dressed and authoritative looking, mostly men of varied ages between about thirty-five and sixty-five, and most were carrying multiple phones to attend to their various responsibilities. Some were paying attention, others looked somewhat disengaged, and one or two were texting. One of the more engaged attendees attempted to correct errors of translation a few times. The trainer laid down explicit 'ground rules' for attendance, such as no lateness and no texting. One attendee asked for the programme of activity and made a request to 'follow the programme', but this was not provided at this stage. Instead, videos were shown showcasing this particular leadership training package as it had been rolled out in an Egyptian hospital and a Nepali health centre (narrated in English). In both cases, the nurses and doctors were depicted as demotivated, disorganised and disinterested, but according to the narrative of the video, following the roll-out of 'The Challenge Model' 'EVERYTHING changed!'.

After a substantial buffet lunch in the hotel restaurant, the workshop proceeded with another video, which was a clip from an Oprah Winfrey show, again in English – the story of Faith the dog. Faith the dog had been born with only two legs, but amazingly had learned to walk on those two legs, to the delight of Oprah and the crowd. This amazing story of perseverance and courage was a lesson for the beginning of the training: *that we do not have problems, but challenges, and challenges can be overcome. Problems are outside, but challenges are something you own.* The trainer went on to show the next video, which explained 'The Challenge Model', which entailed the leadership skill of writing down 'challenges' on a sheet of flip chart paper and listing ways of addressing them, in line with one's mission. This was the basic management model that these leaders would study for the next five days and then roll out to others in their communities around the country to help the fight against malaria.

I did not attend the following days of the workshop but followed up with a number of the attendees in their hometowns across the country. One of the attendees had a master's degree in business from a South African university and ran various business enterprises alongside attending to his religious congregation, being engaged in informal community policing and running a regular meal service for poor children in the city. I asked him what he had got out of 'The Challenge Model'. He thought for a while and said that he had seen such things many times in management textbooks but that it was nice to have practical training on it. As for some of the other participants, he said, they didn't understand so well. He laughed as he described the difficulties in explaining what 'vision' meant in management speak to the local committee. Some argued saying that a vision meant seeing the Prophet. Others argued that vision meant 'seeing', so how could it mean something you think? He acknowledged that for many of them, nothing really had been understood and it was quite superficial. But he would continue and see what happened.

Another attendee, who had asked for the programme at the start of the proceedings, was a priest managing six congregations in a peri-urban area in a northern province. When asked about the usefulness of the programme, he said that there was an issue with the programmes on the ground. He said that people had had big expectations when they saw the NGO cars arrive, and the NGO was giving everything for the leadership training, but not enough was provided to make it work. They needed motorbikes to travel between communities to spread messages about malaria but didn't have them. They had been given US$100 at the district level for stationery and materials – on my calculation, this was about half the cost of a single night's stay in the capital for the international NGO project intern. The lack of resources at the district level to execute plans was a common complaint amongst the members, which went into reports but never seemed to reach the national level. He explained that the transport was needed because usually priests did an exchange – the congregation didn't find it strange that it was another priest from another church talking about malaria. They needed a new face, so they would listen and believe, but they had to trust the face as well. Wryly, he joked that using 'The Challenge Model' they would redirect some of the funding towards transport costs or where they needed to spend it.

***

Very little that I had read in the literature on intervention thus far had primed me to understand what was going on here, which was nonetheless part of a flagship programme in international development and capacity-building. Why would the interveners spend so much money on a programme which was unevenly translated to its intended beneficiaries, who then did not have the resources or infrastructure at the ground level to make it work? Why would the interveners argue – and then say to the experienced, often qualified, assembled community leaders – that their problem was a lack of leadership capacity? How could they liken such leaders to a two-legged dog? And why would such leaders attend this kind of programme? What did this contribute to the strengthening of public services and institutions? Why did complaints about the lack of resource at the local level go nowhere? Were these aspects only a technical problem of programme design and implementation? Or was there something else going on here?

As the research continued, I heard similar stories and issues raised all over the country. This suggested the answers to the questions were likely structural in nature, and these and other problems were widely understood by both interveners and targets of intervention. Moreover, the problems also seemed deeply political, in the sense of turning on highly uneven sets of identities, entitlements and power relations between interveners and their targets. They articulated a particular kind of world view about who and what was to blame for poverty and the nature of state incapacity in the global South, which incidentally seemed at odds with the realities on the ground. Finally, this political structure clearly also resulted in significant patterns of both material accumulation and dispossession – whilst some were doing well materially out of these systems of intervention, it was always clear that this money might have been spent differently, and perhaps with better effects.

***

Working through these problems, this book concludes that interventions fail – *and keep failing* – because they are constituted through structural relations of colonial difference which intimately shape their conception, operation and effects. This interpretation emerges from an examination of the underlying dynamics of hierarchical presence,[2] disposability, entitlement and dependency which characterise intervention. Such tendencies continuously undermine the attempts to centralise capacity within the state and promote wider forms of development and good governance.

Addressing 'failure' is then not a question of Western interveners and scholars finding another technique for 'fixing failed states' through better sequencing, more cultural appropriateness, more hybridity, more participatory planning mechanisms and so on. Nor can it be smoothed by more empathy or better social relations between interveners and targets. When all of these measures are constitutively structured by unacknowledged relations of colonial difference, they will simply produce small variations in this failure, rather than confronting the underlying dynamic itself. This underlying dynamic is a set of constitutive assumptions regarding who is entitled to what in the world (and who is to blame for failure), rooted in forms of common sense which naturalise such inequalities of wealth and power.

The book reaches these conclusions through taking seriously the interpretations and experiences of the targets of intervention – those people whose political systems and livelihoods are supposed to be transformed by the expertise and assistance of international assistance. In Mozambique, whilst there have been 'internationals' of various kinds for centuries, the period after the end of the war in 1990 has seen a particularly large cohort active in the country promoting peace, development, democracy, good governance and so on. Whilst interveners tend to come and go after a few months or years, however, the targets of intervention remain to welcome the next batch and repeat the cycles of co-operation. What does the politics of intervention look like after two or three decades to them?

EXPLORING THE POLITICS OF INTERVENTION

This book uses the term 'intervention' as a shorthand for what are sometimes called 'international statebuilding interventions' which incorporate aspects of development, peacebuilding, good governance promotion and general capacity-building in 'fragile states' and conflict situations in the global South. Whilst there are literatures in different scholarly disciplines, from public administration to peace studies to agricultural sciences, that contribute to discussions about *what* should be done in such situations, this book contributes to an ongoing conversation which seeks to *explain and interpret the political form and significance of intervention.*

Within International Relations (IR), and conflict and peace studies, this debate has taken the form of debates on the 'liberal peace', peacebuilding, post-war reconstruction, international statebuilding and international trusteeship.[3] Unsurprisingly, many of the contributions to the IR debates have zeroed in on questions of sovereignty – in some senses, the 'master' concept of IR. Many contextualise the sovereignty question in terms of the moral and political legitimacy of intervention, its role in maintaining international order and the promotion of specifically liberal norms. Some of the research particularly focuses on the imperial 'paradox' of international governance in a territory which is designed to lead to sovereignty and state strengthening, but which has to undermine sovereignty to do so; whilst some see this as in principle feasible and necessary, others do not.[4]

A specific and important strand of this debate examines the intersection of intervention and globalisation – in particular, the emergence of a global neoliberal economic and political orthodoxy, driven by the West, which has been reformatting all states but particularly those in the global South. In these arguments, sovereignty no longer marks a state boundary but is now articulated as a frontier, in which there is a blurring of regulatory and administrative spaces and responsibilities. In these approaches intervention is fundamentally about the production of global liberal governance, centred around international institutions such as the World Bank.[5]

Another strand of the literature, often ethnographic and practitioner-oriented in terms of its methods, to some extent influenced by critical development studies, has sought to analyse and deconstruct the spaces and practices of international intervention, with a view to talking about how these condition the outcomes of intervention on the ground.[6] In focusing on the gaps between policy and practices, they have not always focused on developing a wider argument about the broader political significance of interventions. However, these works have contributed to the debate by refocusing the gaze of the analyst on the lived experiences of interventions, particularly through the multiple ways in which interveners and targets negotiate the space of intervention, through forms of accommodation, resistance, avoidance, performance and simulation. This has had the consequence of opening up the gaps between policy and practice for scrutiny, shedding light on the imaginaries of interveners, the bureaucratic and physical worlds in which they live and opening up the political logics therein. It has also offered a sensibility which is more attuned to the ways in which power and legitimacy are expressed and mediated in intervention contexts.

The contribution of this book to the debates on the politics of intervention is twofold. First, it seeks to articulate and address the reductive treatment in much of the analysis of the intended beneficiaries, or whom I call the 'targets' of intervention.[7] I argue this is not a methodological accident but emblematic of diverse forms of intellectual Eurocentrism within scholarly research. Counteracting these involves specific strategies for decolonising research, focused on recovering the targets of intervention as political beings. I explain the choice of the term 'target' later in this chapter.[8]

Second, this book builds an alternative explanation of the international phenomenon of intervention upwards from the experiences, interpretations and historical conditions of these targets. Whilst this explanation has significant points of congruence with the existing studies, it suggests a number of other dynamics which embed questions of sovereignty, imperialism and governance *within* deeper hierarchical historic structures of coloniality which nonetheless strongly condition the present order and regimes of intervention. By taking these constitutive structures into account, the apparent failures and limitations of intervention, as well as the experiences of it on the ground, become more intelligible as political phenomena. This then also reframes some of the possible responses in terms of political action. Specifically, it elicits the need for a political ethics of international assistance focused on questions of responsibility, justice and reparation, which can counteract the relations of disposability and dependency embedded in contemporary intervention regimes.

DECOLONISING INTERNATIONAL RELATIONS

How do you 'decolonise' a discipline once characterised by one of its founders as the study of 'the best way to run the world from positions of strength'?[9] Indeed, the primary assumption of contemporary IR – that we live in a world of more or less independent states – in one sense fundamentally presupposes the already-existing success of decolonisation. What does it mean to say this assumption is wrong? And how would one proceed with the study of world politics after that?

For the last twenty years or so, a number of contributions have been made in the field which unearth the past and present of its colonial origins, objects of study, methodological approaches, ethics and zones of exclusion or silence.[10] In this sense, a clear case has been made for IR as a colonial discipline in its constitution, even when we look at its traditional concerns such sovereignty, war, nationalism, international law, international institutions, trade, human rights, democracy and so on.

Within these debates, the organising principles of race and empire and their ongoing significance in the present are being excavated, demonstrated and engaged as political issues. Such work expresses a wider engagement with the histories and politics of decolonisation, the contributions of anti-colonial and postcolonial thought in the twentieth century and a political context in which questions of empire – this time for the United States – were reintroduced into public discussion. In short, this productive line of thinking has brought a number of forgotten histories back into view.

However, the 'decolonising' element of this question calls for more. Specifically, it calls for scholars to engage, examine, retrieve and cultivate *other* ways of thinking about and being in the world that can form alternative points of departure to the hegemonic knowledges of empire. The central aim must be to reject the assumed ways in which global humanity is intellectually ordered into a hierarchy of 'advanced' and 'backward' groups, along lines produced by historic systems of colonial exploitation and dispossession. This means rethinking world politics in terms of its histories, geographies, economies, ecologies, conceptions of the human, the social, the sacred and the mundane and so on. This requires thinking about the kinds of research methods and models to be used and the kinds of constituencies for and with whom the research might be produced (Sabaratnam 2011).

Whilst this is difficult, luckily we as scholars do not have to start from scratch. Once we accept the need to think otherwise, the world is full of already-existing possibilities. Whilst many of these ways of thinking were forged in and through the historical experiences and connections of empire, others have survived them over a longer period.[11] These different ways of dealing with the human condition, often but not always cultivated through experiences of suffering and de-personification, reframe questions of the political, power, justice and ethics in ways which do not take the current state of the world for granted.

Neither do we have to abandon the terrain of substantive explanation and analysis in the search for different points of departure. One widespread characterisation of postcolonial thought – in my view erroneous – has been that its embrace implies a dialogue-inhibiting form of philosophical relativism that precludes convincing analysis. On the contrary, an embrace of the postcolonial question can considerably strengthen and enrich understandings of the world we live in, in terms intelligible to existing philosophies of social science but which challenge its exclusionary starting points (Go 2016). Articulating what Go calls a 'perspectival realism' in the pursuit of global social theory, 'decolonising' our study of the international holds out a substantive promise for more widely enriching our understanding of the causes and dynamics of international order, if those are the questions of common interest.

This book makes a contribution to the project of decolonising IR in three ways. The first is demonstrating, through the extended treatment of a contemporary 'real-world' phenomenon – international statebuilding interventions – that the need and possibilities for decolonising the study of world politics does not need to be, principally, an exercise in history. Finding out that the progenitors of the discipline in the twentieth century were racist colonisers is important, but finding out that the contemporary aid regime operates on racialised hierarchies of entitlement presents a more timely opportunity for demanding change.

The second contribution is its excavation of a theoretical debate informed by specific traditions of critical thinking in IR – broadly put, liberal, Marxist, Foucauldian and constructivist – which maps and interrogates their Eurocentric tendencies. Such an exercise, whilst focused on the specific topic of intervention, has been demonstrated as useful for opening up lines of thinking within other topics characterised by similar debates. Whilst these traditions can all contribute to projects of global justice, without serious attention to the people in whose name justice is being pursued as *political subjects* and not mute objects, they are likely to remain constrained in their vision and analysis.

The third contribution made by the book to decolonising IR is through the suggestion, development and implementation of particular decolonising strategies appropriate to the task, informed by anti-colonial thinkers, on the one hand, and feminist standpoint theory, on the other.[12] In this sense it does the work of putting together a toolbox to reframe the politics of intervention, but which might also be used in other contexts and situations where the analytic problems are similar. More than simply 'good social science' – which might be one way of ensuring the inclusion of histories, political interpretations, material conditions in a particular space – the argument makes its strategic choices in the light of specific and asymmetric forms of analytic erasure within the research.

By bringing a decolonising approach to the study of international intervention, this book works through an ostensibly colonial relation of international power – intervention – with analytic methods which are explicitly designed to unpack this dynamic at the level of theory and practice. The interaction of topic and method in this regard is particularly productive, generating an understanding of dynamics which are highly visible and important from the ground but receive less analytic attention amongst scholars than they should.

RESEARCHING INTERVENTION IN MOZAMBIQUE

As previously mentioned, to study international intervention in Mozambique is to study a site where intervention is perceived to have been both relatively successful and pervasive in terms of its reform of the state institutions. It has not received the same level of research coverage in the international state-building literature as more high profile and expensive post-war interventions in Bosnia, Kosovo, Afghanistan and Iraq. Lacking any high-profile post-war justice mechanisms, or dramatic incidents following its elections, this relatively impoverished, Lusophone country on the southern tip of Africa has been nonetheless tagged as a 'donor darling', receiving over 80 per cent of its public budget in aid in the immediate post-war years. Graham Harrison (2004) has also designated it a 'governance state', one in which the World Bank and other institutions have constitutively permeated the state infrastructure and its financial management systems. In this sense it is a 'hard case' of sorts for the contemplation of international intervention as having been unsuccessful.

Research within Mozambique for this project took place in 2008, 2009 and 2014, amounting to about six months' stay in the country in total. I interviewed over 150 people, of whom 22 were not Mozambican, principally in Portuguese, some in English and others in Makua with translation. Interviewees were selected from across the hierarchy of international co-operation, from a minister and senior civil servants to health workers and farmers' associations, as well as those less directly involved such as journalists, civil society organisers, academics and students. I was also invited to directly observe intervention 'events' by various parties. The research covered the sectors of health, governance and agriculture and was carried out in three different provinces in different zones of the country (Maputo, Sofala and Nampula). Interview data was supplemented through access to the national and local press, TV and radio, elite commentaries published in the media, books bought in Mozambique or academic journals, online historical archives, government documents, donor policy and evaluation documents. It is also more widely supported by extended secondary academic sources on African political economy and history, ethnographies of social power and international aid, and studies on the nature and effect of aid.[13]

The research on Mozambique here is used as a basis for engagement with both individual and shared understandings of international intervention since the end of the war in 1990, rooted in a historical appreciation of ideas of political order, identity and conceptions of justice within the space. This necessarily also involves an engagement with a wide range of questions from agricultural economics to the history of the liberation struggle, to cosmologies of sorcery and witchcraft. The claim of this book is not to have rendered such things authoritatively or completely on their own terms. However, it does aim to provide an account of international intervention as seen through and with these factors.[14] To this extent, the empirical material forms an important part of the argument, even if not in any sense surprising to those familiar with Mozambique or other aid settings. Its contribution is in the disclosure of alternative bases for interpreting the political significance of intervention.

Throughout the book I refer to people in Mozambique as the 'targets' of international intervention. On the one hand, I wish to avoid the language of 'beneficiaries', widely used in policy and implementation documents, as it presupposes positive effects of intervention analytically, which often turn out not to be the case. It also implies a direction of agency from intervener to beneficiary which renders the latter as passive. Other possible formulations, such as 'the local', can also presuppose a particular significance about the political dynamics which to some extent pre-empts the analytic case, as I explain further in chapter 2.

On the other hand, in using the language of 'targets', I also avoid the language of the 'subaltern', popularised in postcolonial thought and in some spaces used to characterise the native subject under colonial rule (Shilliam 2016). One reason is that the term is now (infamously) bound up with a set of debates about interpretive closure and access to languages of power in which this work does not directly intervene. Under the conditions in which this work took place, my interlocutors would not always fit the description of 'subaltern' in relation to our discussions of intervention. However, the use of the term 'targets' is also a positive choice as a descriptor fitting the structural relations of intervention that I am trying to depict. Practices of intervention need to be guided by an idea of the objects of intervention – those people or institutions that are to be transformed. However, to name these people as 'targets' is to leave open the significance and effects of their being targeted. It allows them to be positioned within the political relationship without prejudging a particular analytic outcome.

STRUCTURE OF THE BOOK

The book is structured into two sections. Part I makes a theoretical and methodological argument about how and why 'decolonising' the study of intervention is necessary. It begins in chapter 2 with an account of the recent history of policy and debates on statebuilding, which had to contend with the accusation that such projects were 'imperial' in character. The chapter then expands into a discussion of how even 'critical' accounts of these relations have been excessively Eurocentric in their analyses. By this, I mean that they have consistently focused on the 'West' and interveners as the central object and subject of politics, whilst erasing, avoiding or objectifying any engagement with the targets of intervention as subjects in their own right.

Chapter 3 then seeks to remedy this exclusion by developing 'decolonising strategies' for research, based on the anti-colonial thought of Du Bois, Césaire, Fanon and Cabral. It identifies three useful methods for overcoming the forms of erasure identified in the literature – a recovery of historical presence, an engagement of political consciousness and an investigation of the material conditions of the targets of intervention. It reinforces the analytic prospects of these strategies through a discussion of feminist standpoint theory and its claims for greater scientific objectivity when researching political phenomena 'from below'.

In Part II, these strategies are put into practice, in three extended illustrative discussions of intervention in Mozambique on the state, the peasantry and the politics of anti-corruption. Chapter 4 looks at the effects of international intervention on the functioning of the state – the ostensible object of statebuilding. It does this through an account of what has happened to the health sector, as seen, narrated and experienced by those on the ground. The chapter argues that although public services have visibly improved since the end of the war due to international support, in key respects the state has been 'unbuilt' and fragmented by aid, which targets link to structural problems of impoverishment, aid dependency and donor *protagonismo*.

Chapter 5 narrates the effects of international intervention on the peasantry and agricultural sector, focusing on Nampula Province. Building on the narratives of farmers and agricultural workers, it argues that intervention has refrained from supporting policies that would provide crucial material support to peasant farmers, particularly through the state, meaning that for many farmers engaging with the activities they and the state promote is a risky business. It situates this tendency as a manifestation of the historic structural indifference to the conditions of smallholder farmers since colonial times, rooted in a sense of their political and economic disposability.

Our final illustration looks at the politics of anti-corruption in Mozambique as a means of exploring the limits and blind spots of intervention. Chapter 6 argues that there are multiple ways of thinking about and explaining the problems of corruption in the country, of which technocratic 'good governance' approaches are a small and relatively contained part. More popular and powerful are ways of thinking about contemporary corruption through the icon of Samora Machel, first president of independent Mozambique, famed for his zero-tolerance attitude to corruption, and ideas which link corruption fundamentally to questions of greed, appetite and social equity. In this wider intellectual framework, although international intervention supports anti-corruption activities, its own expensive, wasteful and pro-wealth character is understood to be a contributor to the cultures of corruption which have emerged over the last thirty years.

The concluding discussion in chapter 7 brings together the key findings of the book to ask what they disclose about the politics of international intervention. This chapter argues that it is difficult to make sense of international intervention as a 'bad fit' for 'local' contexts, a grand project of global neoliberal governance or a set of faulty bureaucratic and social practices. Instead, we need to make sense of and explain the asymmetric tendencies which persistently cause it to fail, despite widespread knowledge of its problems. The concepts of the 'coloniality of power' and 'relations of colonial difference' are used to provide useful interpretive and explanatory purchase regarding the constitutive structures of contemporary statebuilding interventions, through developing a connection between the epistemic and material impacts of Western-centrism at the global level and the concrete practices of intervention. Whilst most discussions of these concepts are relatively abstract, they appropriately illuminate and explain the dynamics of *protagonismo*, dependency and disposability identified within the case. With this framework in mind, the conclusion discusses the difference a decolonising political ethics of intervention might make. It offers three suggestions for how interveners could make their policies and practices less immediately destructive, whilst acknowledging that a more fundamental, decolonising change in attitudes, practices and structures is necessary to realise any long-term emancipatory potential.

NOTES

1. This figure is taken from IMF (2007: 10).

2. What will be discussed and characterised as *protagonismo* in chapter 4.

3. An introduction to this debate is available in Campbell et al. (2011). Significant monographs on this topic include Chandler (1999, 2004, 2010b), Duffield (2001, 2007), Paris (2004), Chesterman (2004), Richmond (2005, 2011, 2014), Zaum (2007), Pouligny (2006), Heathershaw (2009), Autesserre (2010, 2014), Hameiri (2010), Mac Ginty (2011). Important edited volumes include Chesterman et al. (2005), Pugh et al. (2008), Lémay-Hebert (2009), Richmond et al. (2009), Call et al. (2009), Campbell et al. (2011), Tadjbakhsh (2011), Richmond et al. (2011) Turner et al. (2014) and Turner et al. (2015).

4. See, for example, Paris (2010) in defence of liberal peacebuilding, against the critical approaches.

5. Governance arguments are most strongly associated with Harrison (2004), Duffield (2007), Hameiri (2010, 2014), Williams (2008, 2013), Zanotti (2011).

6. The most significant of the ethnographic approaches to peacebuilding, state-building and aid within IR are Pouligny (2006), Heathershaw (2009), Lémay-Hebert (2011), Iñiguez-de-Heredia (2012, 2017), Autesserre (2014) and Smirl (2015). These draw some influence from a longer tradition of this work within anthropology and development studies, particularly Ferguson (1990), Chambers (1997), Mosse (2004), Mosse et al. (2011).

7. I would largely exclude Pouligny's excellent account of *Peace Operations Seen from Below* (2006) from this comment. Her work articulates a sociological grounding for reading the operation of power from below and contains striking commentary on the significance of how the UN functions in post-war contexts. Her conclusions on how they are perceived and why strongly resonate with my findings of interveners in the longer term. However, her account of the political stakes does not fully elaborate some of the key issues articulated in this book.

8. With this in mind, I deliberately avoid the language of 'beneficiaries', widely used in policy and implementation documents, as it presupposes positive effects of intervention analytically (and also often turns out not to be the case). Other formulations, such as 'the local' can also presuppose a particular significance about the political dynamics which also, to some extent, pre-empts the analytic case. For these reasons, I have settled on the language of 'targets' of intervention as suitable for the analysis of this book.

9. E.H. Carr, in his 1977 correspondence to Stanley Hoffman, quoted in Haslam (2000: 252–253).

10. Significant contributions include Doty (1993), Krishna (1993), Darby et al. (1994), Grovogui (1996), Barkawi and Laffey (1999, 2002, 2006), Vitalis (2000, 2015), Inayatullah and Blaney (2003, 2010), Long and Schmidt (2005), Jones (2006), Shilliam (2006, 2009, 2011, 2015), Bilgin (2008), Agathangelou et al. (2009), Muppidi (2012), Hobson (2013), Anievas et al. (2014).

11. Examples include Rao (2010), Shilliam (2015), and Pham et al. (2016).

12. See also Julian Go's chapter on the subaltern standpoint (2016: chapter 4).

13. Important sources include Batley (2005), Bozzoli and Brück (2009), Cabrita (2000), de Bragança and Wallerstein (1982), Egerö (1987), Geffray (1990), Gengenbach (2005), Gray (1982), Hall and Young (1997), Hanlon (1984), Henriksen (1978), Honwana and Isaacman (1988), Jone (2005), Marshall (1993), Moreira (1947), Mosca (1999), Newitt (1995), Pitcher (1996, 2006), Vail and White (1980), and Weinstein (2002).

14. The publication of this book is accompanied by a translated summary of its findings in Portuguese, which will be shared and discussed with interviewees and others on a return trip presenting the findings. An online discussion space will be developed at http://meerasabaratnam.com in 2017.

Part I

DECOLONISING CRITIQUE

Chapter Two

Intervention, Statebuilding and Eurocentrism

International interventions in post-war or post-crisis environments are particularly interesting spaces for studying global politics – that is, questions of power, authority, legitimacy, representation, distribution, sovereignty and so on, as enacted between different countries and peoples. To explain why we need to *decolonise* the study of intervention, however, we need to identify its existing 'colonial' parameters. This chapter argues that existing studies of intervention and statebuilding have tended to locate and understand its politics primarily with respect to the power, activities, presence, intentions and policies of Western interveners. Although it has successfully questioned their role, even in 'critical' accounts there are many manifestations of Eurocentrism in how 'politics' is defined and located. This generates an impasse within critique. Despite the recent 'local turn' and 'everyday turn' in the research on intervention, the targets of intervention remain located as mute objects or data points rather than serious interlocutors with an alternative standpoint or traditions of knowledge. In this sense, most scholars and analysts have not yet seriously attempted to 'study up' from the experiences and perspectives of target societies.[1]

I begin the chapter with a brief overview of the now extensive scholarly debates on post-war intervention and statebuilding (which I now simply refer to as 'intervention' for simplicity). Already burgeoning towards the end of the 1990s in peacebuilding circles, the invasions of Afghanistan and Iraq by Western armies prompted a much wider interest in the problem in the Western academy, as well as a much larger response which drew on and developed various critical theoretical resources in IR. In the main part of the chapter I argue that various exemplars of critical accounts of international intervention are constrained by various forms of Eurocentric thinking about Western and non-Western subjects. Such forms of thinking constitutively ignore, bypass or depoliticise the targets of intervention. In the final part of the chapter, I look at how attempts to correct for some of these problems have nonetheless revealed a depth of alignment with intervention as a political practice that strongly permeates the analysis. These arguments pave the way for decolonising strategies informed by standpoint approaches, which are explained in chapter 3.

THE BEGINNER'S GUIDE TO NATION-BUILDING[2]

It seems a commonplace now amongst Western policymakers and many intellectuals that the most obvious answer to war, crisis, famine, disaster, terrorism and poverty in the global South is more and better governance via international statebuilding, but this was not always the case.[3] This specific way of labelling interventions emerged over the last twenty-five years, in which certain circumstances, abilities and ideologies converged, enabling the coalescing of contemporary intervention practices around this idea.[4] Scholarly literature became not only a part of this emerging common sense but also a site in which it was contested.

The field of peace studies had been suppressed during the Cold War in much of the West as politically suspect, as much of it was connected to or informed by an opposition to Western and global militarism. With the end of the Cold War, the immediate upswing in international peacekeeping and peacebuilding missions (see Boutros-Ghali 1992) allowed peace studies scholars into the limelight, particularly to lead discussions on how reconciliation, rehabilitation and reconstruction should be conducted in 'war-shattered' societies (Crocker et al. 1996; Kumar 1997; Lederach 1997; Pugh 2000).

At the same time, there was a growing interest in the problem of failed states (Helman and Ratner 1992), 'good governance' for economic policy (Williams and Young 1994) and the idea of human security through development (UNDP 1994). The neat silos in which security, development, peace, economics, human rights and so on had been contained began to break down via a common focus on governance and the role of the state in delivering goods and services (Duffield 2001). This was informed by a growing academic discourse on state failure and state collapse (Zartman 1995). Emblematically, in 1995 UN Secretary General Boutros Boutros-Ghali issued a *Supplement* to the *Agenda for Peace*, which underscored the need to radically reimagine intervention beyond its limited peacemaking mandate:

> It means that international intervention must extend beyond military and humanitarian tasks and *must include the promotion of national reconciliation and the re-establishment of effective government.* (1995: §13; emphasis added)

This was a significant moment in which the UN's apparent Cold War reluctance to intervene in political affairs was openly jettisoned, in favour of an embrace of all kinds of reforms and transformations to defeat the scourge of state failure and war.

In much of the policy-oriented academic literature, this led to discussion about intervention technique and sequencing. One of the most influential thinkers of this period, Roland Paris, argued that liberalisation reforms should occur only *after* institution-building had taken place (1997, 2004). This was an argument not only for statebuilding but also for protracted, carefully controlled statebuilding. It corresponded historically with the kinds of extended international transitional administration taking place in Bosnia, Kosovo and East Timor, as well as the unfolding chaos in Iraq and Afghanistan, following the US-led invasions in 2001 and 2003, respectively. Others contributed reflections on how and why interventions could work to promote not only internal stability but also wider global order, including in the fight against terrorism (Rotberg 2003; Fukuyama 2004; Call and Wyeth 2008; Ghani and Lockhart 2009).

The founding of the *Journal of Intervention and Statebuilding* in 2006–7 thus coincided with the high point of political and academic activity around the questions of how what was now called intervention and statebuilding would work. However, it also responded to a thread of scholarly literature which had been critical of the politics of international statebuilding from a variety of angles, particularly its resonances with imperial trusteeship. This resonance was picked up by Chandler (1999), Duffield (2001, 2007), Bain (2003), Caplan (2005), Hill (2005), Richmond (2005), Zaum (2007), Mac Ginty (2010) and many others in the ensuing debates. Not all of these thinkers thought this was inherently problematic for the project; some concluded that it was a necessary structure that needed to be embraced for the good of post-war populations in the absence of proper government (Caplan 2004; Zaum 2007).

Others, however, took this critique more seriously and argued that it implied serious ethical and political challenges for the project of intervention. It is to these 'anti-imperial' critical readings that the rest of this chapter now turns. They are interesting not only in terms of their own content but also as representatives of critical-theoretic approaches to the study of IR. Such approaches are mindful of two well-known principles in the critical study of IR: First, that all theories are attached to some particular purpose (Cox 1981) and that their ontologies selectively tell a story about what politics is and where to look for it (Walker 1993). Second, as a consequence, they also – however provisionally – close down possibilities, telling us what is not possible.

If it is true that the critical literature is systematically Eurocentric in various ways, it is also true that it must close down some ways of thinking about the world.[5] It is of course perfectly possible to mount a thoroughly Eurocentric attack on imperialism, and there are long legacies of this kind of thinking in IR (Hobson 2012: 234–284). However, as Gruffydd Jones (2006) has argued, fully comprehending the ways in which imperialism may be a constitutive feature of the international requires a reckoning with the habituated Eurocentric patterns of disciplinary knowledge, including prevalent critical theories, methods and arguments. To this end, this book seeks to 'decolonise' critique by reversing some of its key assumptions.

WHAT IS EUROCENTRISM AND HOW DOES IT LOCATE THE POLITICAL?

Although Eurocentrism has multiple incarnations, overall, it can be described as the sensibility that *Europe is historically, economically, culturally and politically distinctive in ways which significantly determine the overall character of world politics*. As a starting point, we might regard it as a conceptual and philosophical framework that informs the construction of knowledge about the social world – a foundational epistemology of Western distinctiveness. Overall, within Eurocentric sensibilities, 'Europe' is a cultural-geographic sphere (Bhambra 2009: 5), which can be understood as the genealogical foundation of 'the West'. Ascione and Chambers (2016: 303) argue that over time, this has morphed from a view of Europe as the supreme force in world history to a view of Europe as *prima inter pares* while retaining its ontological claim as the generative centre of modernity.

In his piece 'Eurocentrism and Its Avatars', Immanuel Wallerstein (1997) argues that many critical literatures in world history nonetheless reproduce tropes of Eurocentrism in their analyses. Here I suggest these avatars be grouped under three broad headings: culturalist, historical and epistemic. For thinking about where the politics of intervention is 'located', it is necessary to unpack these forms of Eurocentric thinking and reflect on how they shape contemporary scholarly debates.

Some of Eurocentrism's culturalist avatars, as identified by Wallerstein (1997), are now relatively well recognised by scholars across various disciplines. The most famous is probably Orientalism, which is a framing of the East through negative and/or feminised stereotypes of its culture, political character, social norms and economic agency. This framing casts it as a space of tradition and opportunity to be governed and explored, or alternatively feared, by the rational and enlightened West (Said 2003 [1973]). This is closely allied to the avatar of civilisational thinking, which assigns to the West as a whole a package of secular-rational, Judeo-Christian, liberal democratic tolerant social values, in contrast to other civilisations such as the 'Indic' (Wallerstein 1997: 97–98). However, this culturalist avatar seems to have taken new forms since the apparent decline of public Orientalism. As Balibar (1991) has suggested, there are important functional continuities between old and new frameworks based on 'civilisation', 'race' and 'cultural difference' in reproducing an idea of Western distinctiveness. Although now rarely supremacist, this culturalist form of Eurocentrism is generative: It posits the core ontological difference between the West and its Others as arising from their *distinctive* cultures or civilisations, with major political issues emerging from the question of cultural difference and how to manage this. On this reading, a mismatch of 'cultures' is the location of the political, which is about a negotiation of incompatible value systems.

Eurocentrism also manifests through historical avatars. The first of these is the assumption that Europe is the principal subject of world history, as discussed by the *Subaltern Studies* research group, and especially Chakrabarty (2000). This is the tendency of historians (Hobsbawm is offered as the exemplar) to see the emergence of capitalism and industrialisation in the West as the real driver of history and non-Western societies as either 'outside history' or lagging behind Western historical development. A closely related historical avatar includes the notion of Historical Progress (Wallerstein 1997: 96), as elaborated in much post-Hegelian theory, which understands human history as not just linear but also self-consciously improving the human condition through the trying out of different political ideas. Again, these particular forms are understood as somewhat outmoded in scholarship, although they seem to reappear in new guises.

This tendency is evident not only in proclamations of the 'End of History' (Fukuyama 1989) but also in forms of Marxist thought that endow the West with historical 'hyper-agency' in terms of world-historical development (Anievas et al. 2013; Hobson 2004, 2007, 2012). For Bhambra (2010), the emphasis is on the assumption of 'endogeneity' in the story of the rise of Europe: the idea that European development was self-generating – driven by war, competition, the Enlightenment and technological advances – and then diffused out to the rest of the world via imperial expansion. This thus reinstates Europe as the implicit subject of world history and historical sociology and occludes the contemporaneous and necessary involvement of the wider world in this rise (Barkawi and Laffey 2006). Both old and new historical versions of Eurocentrism understand different parts of the world as more and less 'developed', or more and less 'modern', indicating a strong connection between geographic-cultural space and temporal/scalar positioning (Hindess 2007; Hutchings 2008). What this means is that politics proper, thought of as the evolution of social relations, is focused in global terms on the West as its primary site and agent.

Finally, we can identify Eurocentrism's epistemic avatar, which is the purported atemporal universalism of modern social scientific knowledge (Wallerstein 1997: 100). In this tendency, social scientific modes of knowledge which emerged in Europe from the nineteenth century onwards are represented as supremely privileged in their understanding of social phenomena above other modes of knowing, as demonstrated through their powers of abstraction, reasoning and objectivity. This also establishes a hierarchy of knowers with the authority to speak about the world, which tracks their positions in relation to the Western academy (Smith 1999). Put bluntly, it is an assumption that 'the West knows best', particularly when it comes to critical thinking. Thus, even apparently 'anti-imperial' or 'postmodern' critiques of social science often do not disrupt the overall claims to hegemony of social-scientific or legal knowledge (Mignolo 2002: 86–90) where there is no reckoning with the question of epistemic location or a refusal of anything other than its own universalist claims. This is because such knowledge presents itself as a logically bounded totality.

Yet, there is a tension that emerges from what Shilliam calls the 'double hermeneutic'; this is the tension inherent in the claim that, on the one hand, all social beings interpret reality, but, on the other hand, scholastic interpretations are better than others (2014: 355). As a consequence, one of the ways in which this manifests itself is through the asymmetric casting of doubt on some claims – purported to be 'biased' or 'suspect' – more than others. In an analytic sense, then, these knowledges are often ignored, downgraded and circumscribed – included as 'data points' rather than having any interpretive validity in and of themselves. This habit is particularly pronounced where the other knowers are understood as distant from and culturally 'Other' to Western academic knowledge.

Overall, Eurocentric tendencies in scholarship limit thinking about the world in three identifiable ways: first, where politics is located; second, who knows about it; and third, what kinds of responses are thinkable. To repeat, a general belief in Western historical/epistemic primacy does not necessarily lead to support for an imperialist politics – indeed, as will be discussed, what is interesting is the manifestations of these tendencies in *anti*-imperial work. And none of these accounts are 'crudely' Eurocentric in the sense of being anachronistically Orientalist, racist or triumphalist. Rather, their analyses are often informed by 'cutting' edge critical theory. My argument is that they lead to a limited understanding and explanation of the politics of intervention, a circumscribed sense of the possibilities for connections and solidarities between the West and non-West, as well as a limited articulation of what an anti-imperial politics can look like. Without a substantive alternative to the Eurocentric philosophical terrain upon which the debates have taken place, the critiques themselves may become 'apologia' (Chandler 2010: 137) for what exists rather than grounds for alternative political practices. Thus, whilst much of the work that has emerged is 'indispensable', it is also often 'inadequate', to borrow Chakrabarty's terms (2000).

CRITIQUES OF INTERVENTION AND THE PROBLEM OF EUROCENTRISM

The critical debate on intervention is haunted by five particular avatars of Eurocentrism, which extend from the categories above: a bypassing of target subjects in empirical research; the analytic bypassing of subjects in frameworks of governmentality; an ontology of cultural Otherness distinguishing the 'liberal' from the 'local'; the analytic constraints of 'everyday' approaches; and nostalgia for the liberal social contract, the liberal subject and European social democracy. These collectively generate an impasse in which Western liberalism is not only seen as a source of oppression but also implicitly rehabilitated as the only true source of emancipation. As such, the critical approaches developed hitherto cannot imagine a world in which the targets of intervention can generate their own meaningful terms of engagement with interveners, nor critically evaluate the problems of modernity and development, rooted in their own experiences and knowledges. In unpacking the manifestations of Eurocentrism in the debate, this section draws attention to the constitutive absence and depoliticisation of the targets of intervention as political subjects.

Bypassing the Targets of Intervention: Research Design

Whilst this is not the trend in much of the more recent critical literature on intervention, in the earlier work which set the research agenda, and in later formulations, there was a tendency to exclude or marginalise consideration of the people targeted by its interventions from the analysis. This methodological exclusion manifested itself in different ways.

In a seemingly banal sense, it manifested often in work which sought to focus principally on the conceptualisation of intervention rather than its specific effects. Thus, some major works in the debate such as Richmond's *Transformation of Peace* (2005) and Chandler's *International Statebuilding: The Rise of Post-Liberal Governance* (2010) did not represent or engage with the activities or behaviour of particular peoples targeted by interventions since these were not considered relevant to the overall framing of this part of the research. Rather, such projects focused on making sense of the genealogies, contradictions and trajectories of intellectual traditions associated with the 'West' as the key object of intellectual concern. In the context of these deliberations, the peoples targeted by intervention were implicitly irrelevant to the conclusions that the research wanted to draw about the West's relationship with post-conflict environments. Whilst this is a methodological 'exclusion', then, it does not on the surface appear a problematic one – rather, it seems a natural artefact of a research design focused on Western ideology.

Contributing to the theoretical framing, methodological exclusion of targeted peoples also characterised some of the empirical work on particular interventions. This often focused very largely on the policies, beliefs and practices of interveners. Exemplary of this were Chandler's *Faking Democracy after Dayton* (1999) and *Empire in Denial* (2006), which almost exclusively looked at the international administrative structures and their illiberal and hypocritical exercise of power. Where Bosnians did appear it was briefly and through a short explanation of their nationalist voting patterns in the context of anti-corruption policies (2006: 154–157).

This same methodological exclusion is, however, also manifested in other influential writings. For example, in the cases covered in Richmond and Franks' *Liberal Peace Transitions* (2009), the focus is almost exclusively on the trajectory of the interventions. References to Kosovans, Cambodians and Timorese people are relatively brief, generally about recalcitrant politicians and offered in service of a critique that demonstrates the failure of intervention to transform societies. Chesterman (2008) argues that the same applies to Zaum's (2007) treatment of target societies. Even in Duffield's work, which has included substantial efforts to ground the global theoretical critique in particular cases, the overarching tendency is to focus on the interveners and their practices in those environments rather than the peoples targeted by intervention. We see this particularly accentuated in the handling of the Zambezia Road Feeder Project in Mozambique (2007: 82–110) and continuities in Western attitudes towards Afghanistan (133–158). Similarly, Hameiri's excellent analysis (2010) of the production of regulatory statehood through statebuilding in the Asia-Pacific uses several cases but systematically ignores the targets of intervention in the analysis. Again, there is a seemingly solid rationale for this – that this is the right methodological choice to make because these interventions are themselves the object of inquiry.

Yet, it is a fundamental of most philosophies of social science that methodological choices reflect underlying ontological premises (Jackson 2010). As noted, our ontological premises determine our basic understanding of what the political *is* (Walker 1993). In these cases, to look *only* at interveners, and to imply by design that this is an adequate account of the politics of intervention, helps to reproduce, however unintentionally, the background assumption that what is exterior to the interveners does not matter for an appreciation of the politics of intervention. The fact that no explicit methodological rationale is usually offered for this absence suggests further that this is a matter of scholarly common sense.

Thus defining and framing inquiry in this way supports habits of intellectual Eurocentrism by emphasising 'Western' agency as the terrain – or ontology – of the political. What is under question then is not whether the methods used were adequate to the research question, but why research questions about the politics of intervention are continuously framed in this way. On my reading, this methodological habit precisely reproduces tenets of 'old' Eurocentrism here – the implied passivity, irrelevance or mysteriousness of the non-West – even as it tries to avoid them. It is argued that in combination with other avatars of Eurocentrism, it has played an important role in generating a critical impasse within the debate.

Bypassing the Targets of Intervention: Governmentality Approaches

Allied to the methodological exclusion of peoples targeted by interventions is a deeper analytic bypassing of such peoples as substantive political subjects, via critical accounts of global governance. Specifically, the recent critical debate on intervention has also been strongly influenced by the idea that it is a form of liberal governmentality (Dillon and Reid 2000). This is the idea, derived from Foucault, that it is a productive technology of power which seeks to regulate life through its freedom – through the production of self-governing liberal subjects. Global governmentality is understood to operate through a system of biopolitics (Duffield 2005; Richmond 2006), which articulates sovereign power as shifting from a management of territories to a management of bodies. The debate has been unfolding alongside the broader rise of Foucaultian analytics of the international and, particularly, in analyses of war, peace and global governance (Jabri 2007; Joseph 2010).

This analytic framework, particularly as developed by Duffield in the two books cited here (2001, 2007), has been incredibly powerful as a critical imaginary for understanding the structure and practices of the development-security nexus and intervention in the global South. This is a nexus that is seen to have emerged following the realignment of global economic processes, which increasingly exclude the South from relations of production and investment. In doing so, however, they re-include it via relations of liberal governance. Whilst the first book details the emerging strategic complex of actors – humanitarian, military, developmental – who intervene widely in the global South in new configurations, the second rearticulates these practices via a reading of liberal power as the expanding frontier of Western biopolitical governance.

Duffield offers his reading of what he calls 'liberal peace' (2001: 9), through Foucault, as a contrast to theses suggesting that interventions are a 'new imperialism' (2001: 31–34). Rather, liberal power is 'based on the regulation and management of economic, political and social processes' (34). One of the most important themes emerging from the later work (2005, 2007) is the unevenness of life-chances and developmental expectations accorded to the liberal West and the rest of the world. For Duffield this is a continuation of colonial strategies of rule (2005) and liberal racism (2007: 185–214) designed to contain populations globally. Duffield roots this analysis in Harvey's critique of capitalism's need to manage 'surplus populations' to avoid systemic crises (2007: 10–11).

However, the central problem with this analytic framework is its tendency to ignore the exteriority of power through the discounting of Southern subjecthood. This turns on the way in which political power and political subjecthood are implicitly understood to interact and produce consent:

> People in the South are no longer ordered what to do – they are now expected to do it *willingly* themselves. Compared to imperial peace, power in this form, while just as real and disruptive, is more nuanced, opaque and complex. Partnership and participation imply the mutual acceptance of shared normative standards and frameworks. Degrees of agreement, or apparent agreement, within such normative frameworks establish lines of inclusion and exclusion. (Duffield 2001: 34)

Here it is strongly implied that liberal governmentality in the international sphere operates in the way liberal governmentality operates within 'advanced liberal societies' (Joseph 2010: 224) – that is, specifically through the effective and productive power of liberal discourse to produce self-regulating and self-governing subjects. If it is the case that intervention consists of a strategic complexes of governance consisting of different actors (Duffield 2001: 12), then the implication is that they are governing the global South through the production of liberal subjectivity.

Nonetheless, the way Duffield frames it here actually hedges the bet over Southern subjectivity whilst simultaneously endorsing the overall framework. That is, he does not want to say outright that Southern political subjecthood is produced by intervention. Yet, this is the point of the 'governmentality' framework insofar as it has any analytic traction, that is that it is a specific modality of power which works through the production of volition rather than coercion or loyalty. Throughout the work then, we have a fairly strong narrative of intervention and development-security network as a web or network of Western liberal power, the logic of which works through its attempted production of liberal subjects.

There are long-standing debates as to whether a Foucaultian account of power is applicable at a global level (Joseph 2010), adequate for understanding either the development of governmental structures themselves or the nature and character of resistance. As Jabri (2007: 74) notes, postcolonial critiques have argued that Foucault's own focus on the European expression of power ignores the differentiated character of imperial power. In particular, they have problematised Foucault's ignoring of the specific historical angle or positionality that informs his account of power (Jabri 2007: 74) and, subsequently, his account of resistance that is itself ideologically somewhat empty, as noted by Spivak (Jabri 2007: 75).

These concerns can be applied to the use of his work in the intervention debate and are specifically connected to the account of the subject that is implicit in the governmentality framework. Chandler has made similar claims, arguing that there is an emptiness to Duffield's call for a 'solidarity of the governed' as a response to global liberal governmentality (Chandler 2009: 67), because it lacks a political subject as the basis for critical theorising (2010: 153).

Chandler is right, to an extent; there *is* a lack of political subjecthood in Duffield's account of intervention. However, what he does not clearly specify is that the principal lack is of the subjecthood of those *targeted* by intervention, not those seen to be enacting it. The latter are given plenty of strategic agency, intentionality, ideology and purpose in this framework. In this sense, Duffield's account of intervention is not dissimilar to Chandler's, in that they both focus on the agency and subjecthood of interveners, even if under the analytic of governmentality this becomes more diffuse. Yet, they both exclude and avoid considerations of the exteriority of this power, and particularly the peoples targeted by interventions as political subjects. The habit of methodological exclusion noted in the previous section becomes then cognate with the analytic exclusions which underpin the framework of governmentality. Both exhibit avatars of Eurocentrism, which emphasise the distinctiveness and importance of Western behaviour and primacy whilst occluding the space outside it.

Ontologies of Otherness: Liberal-Local Relations, Hybridity and Resistance

Sensitive to the problem of such occlusion, a major strand of recent literature has emphasised the need to rethink the relations between the 'liberal' and the 'local' in intervention settings (Mac Ginty 2011; Richmond 2009, 2010, 2011), in what has been labelled a 'fourth-generation' approach (Richmond 2011), or 'the local turn' (Mac Ginty et al. 2013). This writing has taken a much more proactive approach to research with and about the peoples targeted by intervention, aiming to correct the impression of smooth liberal transformation and the 'romanticisation' of the local (Mac Ginty 2011: 2–4). Yet the paths it has taken have, inadvertently, reinforced a Eurocentric understanding of intervention, through using an ontology of 'Otherness' to frame the issues. This is despite attempts to acknowledge or engage with the 'colonial' resonances of peacebuilding and 'postcolonial' ideas.

Prominent amongst these accounts is Richmond's recent work on the 'liberal peace' (2005, 2006) and 'post-liberal peace' (2009, 2010, 2011), which frames the key problems of intervention through an ontological distinction between the 'liberal' and the 'local'. In earlier writing, intervention is elaborated as foundationally liberal and genealogically endogenous to 'Western' traditions of thought, reflecting Enlightenment, modern and post-Christian liberal values (Richmond 2005). In post-conflict settings, however, the liberal peace is critiqued for exercising forms of hegemony that suppress pluralism, depoliticise peace, undermine the liberal social contract and exercise a colonial gaze in its treatment of local 'recipients' of intervention. In view of these various aspects of failure, liberal intervention is characterised as 'ethically bankrupt' (2009a: 558) and requiring re-evaluation.

The 'local', on the other hand, is a space characterised by 'context, custom, tradition and difference in its everyday setting' (2010: 669), which is suppressed by interventions. The very conception of the 'post-liberal peace' is thus about the ways in which two ontologically distinct and separate elements – the 'liberal' and 'local' are 'rescued and reunited' via forms of hybridity and empathy, in which 'everyday local agencies, rights, needs, custom and kinship are recognised as discursive "webs of meaning"' (2010: 668).

Mitchell has recently argued that Richmond's conception of the 'local' is not 'a reference to parochial, spatially, culturally or politically bounded places' but 'the potentialities of local agents to contest, reshape or resist within a local "space"' (Mitchell, 2011: 1628). Richmond himself has also been concerned not to be understood as 'essentialising' the 'local', emphasising that it contains a diversity of forms of political society (2011: 1628), including that which is called the 'local-local'. Indeed, this more recent work elaborates a more complex conception of the 'everyday' as a space of action, thought and potential resistance.

Despite these qualifications, however, there is much conflation, interchangeability and slippage between these conceptions of the 'local'. Accordingly, the ontology of Otherness, understood as cultural distinctiveness and alterity, continuously surfaces throughout the narratives of liberal and post-liberal peace. Not only is intervention closely linked to the intellectual trajectory of the 'West', but a conception of the 'local' as non-modern and non-Western often reappears:

This requires that local academies and policymakers beyond the already liberal international community are enabled to develop theoretical approaches to understanding their own predicaments and situations, *without these being tainted by Western, liberal, and developed world orthodoxies and interests.* In other words, to gain an understanding of the 'indigenous' and everyday factors for the overall project of building peace, liberal or otherwise, a via media needs to be developed between emergent local knowledge and the orthodoxy of international prescriptions and assumptions about peace. (Richmond 2009: 571; emphasis added)

There is a clear emphasis here on the need to engage with the 'indigenous' or 'authentic' traditions of non-Western life, which seems to reflects an underlying assumption of *cultural* difference as the primary division between these two parties. This reproduces the division between the liberal, rational, modern West and a culturally distinct space of the 'local'.

Indeed, the call for a post-liberal peace is often a call for peace-building to reflect a more 'culturally appropriate form of politics' (2011: 102) which is more hybrid, empathetic and emancipatory. This emphasis on tradition and cultural norms as constitutive of the 'local' is carried through in recent research on interventions in Timor Leste and the Solomon Islands. These focus largely on the reinvigoration of 'customary' houses and institutions as a form of 'critical agency' in distinction to liberal institutions and the state (2011: 159–182). The point here is not simply that there is an account of alterity or cultural difference within the politics of intervention, but that the liberal/local distinction appears to be *the central ontological fulcrum* upon which the rest of the political and ethical problems sit (see also Chandler 2010: 153). Therefore 'local' or 'everyday' 'agency' is seen to be best expressed to the extent that it reclaims 'the customary' and is not 'co-opted' by the internationals. It is understood as enhanced where codes of 'customary law' become part of the new constitutional settlement.

A similar division can be seen in Mac Ginty's framework, which sees the hybridities in peacebuilding as emerging at the intersection of the 'international' and 'local' agents and institutions (2011). Again, this framework is built on an ontological distinction between the two which repeatedly splits the 'Western'/'international' from the 'non-Western'/'local'. Even though this is well qualified, overall Mac Ginty defends this distinction, arguing that if one were to abandon such potentially problematic labels, then this would lead to an abandonment of research altogether (2011: 94). This can quite straightforwardly be read as a defence of the basic ontology of the project of the 'local turn', which is an ontology of the distinction between the West and its Others, which meet through various forms of hybridisation. Whilst Mac Ginty does not pursue the ethics of the post-liberal peace in the same way as Richmond, the underlying intellectual framework also uses this distinction as the analytic pivot of the research.

We earlier defined Eurocentrism as the belief in Western distinctiveness, and I have argued that this is philosophically fundamental to 'the local turn' in the literature. This point is also picked up by Paffenholz (2015) and Randazzo (2016). This strand has put substantial analytic weight on fundamental cultural differences between these two entities, even whilst disavowing any essentialism and making some substantive conceptual efforts to move away from this. Such difficulties are indicative of the deep hold that this particular avatar of Eurocentrism has on the critical imaginary. By contrast, the point made by a wide variety of other 'postcolonial' writers has precisely been *against* such an ontology of the international, pointing instead to the historically blurred, intertwined and mutually constituted character of global historical space and 'culture' (Bhambra 2009; Nadarajah et al. 2016). Whilst this is occasionally acknowledged, it does not interrupt the direction of argument as such.

The 'Everyday' and Hermeneutic Containment

That said, the turn to the 'everyday' in the literature on intervention is not all reliant on a culturalist or binary ontology of the 'local'. Arguably the most significant recent work in the field of intervention scholarship is Severine Autesserre's *Peaceland* (2014), which is a rich, close ethnographic study of various sites of international intervention. Autesserre draws on the recent 'practice turn' in IR advanced by Pouliot, Adler and others (Bueger et al. 2015), to develop an explanation of the failures of intervention rooted in the everyday practices of interveners including their knowledge practices and daily work routines. *Unlike* other scholars in the 'local turn', she does not root the term 'local' in terms of culture, agency or resistance, but uses it to describe in a positional sense to talk about people targeted by interventions (2014: 64). That is the approach also suggested in this book. Also unlike many of the studies already cited, she does not methodologically bypass those subjects but engages with them and presents their voices in the course of the study, relating them to the wider 'structures of inequality' which characterise *Peaceland* (2014: 194–214). She also declines to characterise intervention as necessarily 'liberal' by design, pointing to the disconnect between the seemingly 'liberal' ideals and its practical dimensions (2014: 52–53). In this sense, Autesserre's research *design* already shows some potential to work against the Eurocentric habits and tendencies in thinking about intervention that we have already identified. In addition, there is much which focuses in on the political tensions between interveners and targets, following in the footsteps of Pouligny (2006).

Autesserre's analysis, however, comes across also as an exercise in the hermeneutic containment of her 'local' interlocutors when it comes to their own analysis, even as she recognises the realities to which they point. In a number of places throughout the analysis, she quotes at length from amongst her interviewees, and these interviewees are explicitly referencing colonialism, imperialism and racism (2014: 74, 100, 216). Yet, she herself systematically declines to take these as serious interpretations, often leaving them unremarked-upon or choosing to interpret them as part of more generic everyday structures of inequality or ineffective daily work practices. In the text there is occasional passing reference to 'postcolonial theory' or scholars, but these questions are never seriously elaborated. Indeed, the presence of African-origin international civilians in peacekeeping missions is implied to *disqualify* intervention as a setting in which colonial or racist relations might obtain (60–61) – as if any institution of colonial governance was established only by whites.

The subsequent analysis conforms to what Debra Thompson characterises as 'racial aphasia' (2013: 44–45) – an inability to speak about race, but in this case also colonialism and imperialism. Subsequently, the nature of the structural 'inequality' between 'internationals' and 'locals' is never fully theorised – it simply 'is' the grounds on which the 'practices' of interveners take place. Rather the 'practices' of interveners become not just a methodological entry point but the primary conclusion of her study into intervention. Autesserre's conclusions and policy recommendations in this sense look and feel a bit strange as she exhorts interveners to try harder to be more reflexive and less exclusionary or estranged in their social practices, but in ways which resonate with their existing priorities for intervention such as security (2014: Conclusion).[6]

For Autesserre, Eurocentric thinking is thus manifest in an ongoing and final epistemic alignment with the international interveners, whose good faith, technical expertise and policy objectives are taken as true, even in the face of the multiple alternative plausible interpretations that are available from her own empirical research as she has herself presented it. That said, one has the sense that throughout the text Autesserre is wrestling with the double hermeneutic discussed by Shilliam – the balance between a fidelity to her interpretive method and findings and the specific need to emerge with a story that aligns with the stories interveners tell about themselves and their motivations. This epistemic alignment, however, ultimately acts as a form of hermeneutic closure in favour of intervention, bypassing these alternative and less flattering interpretations and their significance. Rather, Autesserre's conclusions offer yet another possibility for the deferred redemption of international intervention.

Nostalgia for Social Contract Politics, Welfare Democracy and the Liberal Political Subject

The manifestations of Eurocentrism just discussed are prominent features of critiques which shape the basic starting points of research. This last avatar can, however, be characterised as more 'recessive' in critical scripts, occupying a more muted but important place in the overall thinking. This is an implicit nostalgia for the social contract, the liberal subject and the welfare state, which are understood to provide the substance of many of the alternatives to intervention. However, as will be further elaborated, these end up reinforcing the rationale for interventions rather than disrupting them.

The 'social contract' or even 'liberal social contract' is sometimes invoked in the critiques not only as a means of restoring balance between powerful and less powerful actors, but also as a way of shoring up intervention itself through moving away from neoliberalism. For Richmond, a 'new social contract' offers a means of balancing the international with the indigenous, which provides the basis for a post-liberal peace with more 'everyday legitimacy' (2009: 567–568). For Divjak and Pugh, writing in the context of corruption in post-conflict Bosnia, the main cause of corruption is understood as the 'absence of a liberal social contract' (2008: 373). This resonates with other literature that has pointed to the 'external' rather than 'internal' contract engendered by peacebuilding (Barnett and Zürcher 2009).

This line of argument is interesting precisely because of the strong suggestion that what is required is not a rejection of intervention, but the need to control it by bringing it into a classical liberal framework of accountability through contract. If only such contractarian relations were available to guide international-local relations, or indeed the relations between elites and masses, then intervention could, in Richmond's words, be 'salvaged'. Practitioners might of course point out that in a formal sense there are plenty of 'contracts' and agreements that govern intervention in all peacebuilding missions – governments necessarily consent to them, and constitutions are also forged through political processes which are designed to be 'inclusive'. For critics who know this, however, the implication must be that these are not genuine or authentic forms of contracting.

Complementary to the call for a (better) social contract is also a call for more welfare provision and state intervention in post-conflict economies within a critique of neoliberal economic policy (Pugh 2005, 2009; Richmond 2008). This resonates with Duffield's observation that the provision of 'social insurance' for 'surplus populations' in the global North is not replicated in the South (2007: 217). In particular, Pugh emphasises the need for employment creation and labour rights (2008), and Richmond emphasises the meeting of basic needs and rights through better state provision (2008). These stipulations are both, however, combined with an emphasis on the need to uphold 'culture' or 'heterogeneity' (Pugh et al. 2008) in the context of a developmental political economy and with a consciousness of the problems of some of these objectives (Richmond 2011: 39).

Whilst the critique of the effects of neoliberal economic policy in these writings is very insightful and important, it is nonetheless interesting that the alternative vision is clearly based on a particular conception of state-led social democracy akin to that practised in post-war western Europe, but one which is able to accommodate culturally appropriate modifications and development. Again, however, practitioners might well point to this as actually reflecting the current centre of gravity in intervention policy ('we are all Keynesian now', quoted in Richmond 2011: 169). Moreover, they may note that it is Western donors themselves that have enabled any kind of social provision via health and education services to take place. Whilst critics might argue soundly that such provisions are everywhere inadequate, this does not seem to reflect any kind of real gap in thinking between interveners and critics.

In a slightly different vein, other critiques have shown a nostalgia for the liberal political subject as a basis of political action. Earlier, for example, we noted that Chandler (2010) critiqued Duffield for the thinness of the idea of the 'solidarity of the governed'. In the same piece, Richmond is also criticised for a fear of doing epistemic violence to 'the Other'. These concerns reflect Chandler's criticisms of post-structuralist and cosmopolitan approaches, which mourn the loss of the 'liberal right-bearing subject' (2009: 56) and the 'transformative dynamic ontology of the universal rational subject' (2010: 155).

This is because, for Chandler, intervention does not represent so much the contradictions of divergent strands of liberalism but a degraded 'neoliberal' form which critiques autonomy (2010). Whilst it is never made totally explicit what kind of politics of engagement Chandler would advocate, it is clear that his preoccupations with autonomy, sovereignty and the virtual death of political ideologies in the West indicate a kind of refounded pluralist liberalism in which 'politics' and 'autonomy' are themselves more highly valued as the foundation of a *properly* political project. Yet, as Jones has recently argued, this seems to depend upon an implicit defence of the 'mythology' (Chandler's word) of unproblematic autonomy as the basis for political society (Jones 2011: 237). Indeed, the focus on the unaccountability of intervention and the critique of autonomy suggests that he, too, might be in favour of a classical liberal social contract as the alternative to neoliberalism.

Thus the critiques of intervention often remain tied to alternatives which reflect political imaginaries grounded in the vision of a 'better' European past, either in terms of ideas about the social contract or welfare state or about the autonomous liberal political subject. These imaginaries may all be improvements in many respects on the present situation; however, it is perhaps disconcerting that these alternatives are framed in terms of and with references to such a past and that there is little real difference between these visions and those that practitioners of intervention themselves hold. These are an important limit to the potentiality of critique through confining the intellectual spaces from which critique can emerge.

CONCLUSION

In a recent piece defending liberal peacebuilding, Roland Paris accuses its critics of failing to come up with alternatives to it, arguing that mostly they endorse variants of liberalism, or just nothing at all (2010: 354–357; see also Begby and Burgess 2009). Indeed, in terms of the defence he offers, this is one of the most biting counter-critiques: There Is No Alternative. He is partially right, but for the wrong reasons. The problems emerge not because there is nothing ultimately better than liberalism but because the deeper framework of philosophical Eurocentrism denies the possibility of any real political exteriority to this broad category of ideas. So, even where intervention is understood as a project of global governmentality, the only subjects and agents who appear in the picture are the interveners themselves. Thus for Paris it becomes relatively easy to claim that anything short of self-declared and non-consensual totalitarian colonialism enforced through naked violence is actually some form of – implicitly acceptable – 'liberalism', because there is an intellectual conflation of 'Western' activity with liberal action, and indeed the politics of intervention itself. This converges with Autesserre's sense that whereas colonialism is characterised principally by prejudice and violence (2014: 56), contemporary intervention is not.

This leaves critiques trapped in an impasse, which may be characterised as a 'paradox of liberalism'. On the one hand, the critiques problematise intervention's liberal biopolitics, cultural inappropriateness, neoliberal economic policies and unaccountability, but, on the other, they try to respond to these problems through some kind of middle ground, better practices or some kind of 'proper' liberalism of the past. This is the circle in which interventions and its critics find themselves enclosed, with interventions themselves apparently softening their edges and filling the space through emphases on 'local ownership', 'participatory governance', multidimensional approaches to poverty reduction and political 'partnership' with aid-recipient countries.

These reforms in intervention practice accordingly often overlap with critiques to such an extent that it is unclear whether critiques themselves have only become descriptive, rather than critical, of the present directions in intervention policy (see Millar 2014). Overall, Duffield is consistently more conscious and sceptical of these colonial dimensions of the present security-development nexus (2005) and of the longer entanglements of 'liberal' intervention practices with racism, imperialism and attempts to control the colonial frontier (2007). Others seem to recognise these continuities; yet Richmond cites the creation of the Tribal Liaison Council in Afghanistan as an indication of a hybrid interface between the international and local and the emergence of the 'post-liberal peace' (2009: 337). But is this really something to be celebrated as more 'culturally appropriate', or does it instead represent a more efficient instrument of neocolonial governance?

The critical literature on intervention thus far is characterised in various dimensions by forms of Eurocentric theory, method and conclusion and as such gives us only limited scope for understanding it, or reimagining the nature of intervention and its alternatives. This is so even as this literature produces multiple important insights about its significance, nature and functioning, particularly as it draws empirically closer to how intervention operates in more detail. In the next chapter, I show how our conceptual and methodological grounding can be rethought through strategies for decolonising our understandings.

NOTES

1. Exceptions include Pouligny (2006), Heathershaw (2009), Autesserre (2010, 2014).

2. The title of a book released by the RAND Corporation (Dobbins et al. 2007). Much of this section draws directly on Sabaratnam (2011a) and Heathershaw (2008). See also Cunliffe (2012).

3. A contrary, and important, reading of the place of statebuilding operations is put forward by Shahar Hameiri, who locates it not in the changes in peacebuilding practice but as part of a wider schema of global governance via the regulation of statehood (Hameiri 2013; Hameiri et al. 2015).

4. This is, of course, not to deny the historical resonances and continuities in terms of content with broader projects of colonial and postcolonial development, which privileged the standing of external experts and models, and to which my argument will return; rather, it is to locate the contemporary idea of 'international statebuilding' as a specific discourse of recent heritage, with a particular rationale.

5. This argument draws directly on Sabaratnam (2013) and extends it with regard to the most recent literature.

6. See also review by Carayannis (2015).

Chapter Three

Strategies for Decolonising Intervention

So, what is to be done? The Eurocentric tendencies in much of the present literature place limits on how we understand international intervention. As noted in the previous chapter, these tendencies work in different ways, and many of them are 'anti-imperial' in their sensibilities. However, they have the collective effect of heavily circumscribing the ontological and epistemological bases of critique. This is because they depoliticise the 'local' targets of intervention and their significance and reinscribe interventions and interveners themselves as the 'true subjects' of international politics. This not only creates a tension between their objectives and their methods, in some cases, but more fundamentally impoverishes the wider scholarly and public debates on intervention.

This chapter develops strategies for researching intervention from a 'decolonising' orientation, grounded both in the historical project of decolonisation and in scholarly debates about knowledge production. This chapter articulates a set of principles on which to base research, as well as a philosophical grounding for the kind of approach advanced. The effect of these strategies is, first, to reconstruct the presence of target societies within the analysis and, second, to provide a rationale for how and why these might support an alternative explanation for the politics of intervention. This approach forms the basis for the analysis across the three subsequent chapters, each of which deals with an aspect of intervention in post-war Mozambique.

This chapter begins with a look at the historical project of decolonisation in the twentieth century through the work of W. E. B. Du Bois, Aimé Césaire, Frantz Fanon and Amílcar Cabral. These thinkers all contributed actively to the politics as well as the intellectual basis for decolonisation in/of Africa, and all developed intellectual strategies to counteract discourses of colonial rule. Whilst contemporary manifestations of Eurocentrism in research on intervention are in a number of ways distinct from early twentieth century justifications for colonialism, there is a common structure to the intellectual framing of hierarchy, exclusion and presence which means that mapping techniques for dealing with colonialism onto Eurocentrism should be a productive way forward. The three strategies for the reconstruction of target societies which I borrow from these thinkers are a recovery of historical presence, an engagement with the political consciousness of subordinate actors and an appreciation of the material conditions in which they operate.[1]

The second part of the chapter engages with the debate around feminist standpoint approaches to the analysis of society. I argue that this provides a set of important rationales for why research on society is improved and made more 'objective' by engaging with the experiences and consciousness of those in subordinate positions, as also recommended by decolonising strategies. In this section, questions of representation, positionality, objectivity and epistemic privilege are discussed and clarified in relation to common critiques. This move is important in terms of underscoring the significance of the *methodological* challenge posed by these approaches to *all* research, even for those who are sceptical about the associated projects of anti-sexism and anti-racism to which feminist and decolonising strategies are often attached.

STRATEGIES FOR RECONSTRUCTING SUBJECTHOOD

In the previous chapter it was argued that intervention scholarship was characterised by varied manifestations of Eurocentrism – the tendency to mark the West as the proper subject of political analysis, with 'other' people and societies (i.e. the targets of intervention) as analytically subordinate. To think against Eurocentrism, we need strategies to counteract this subordination. This is not to say that the reconstruction of subaltern subjects in and of itself delivers an adequate response, but it is a necessary starting point (Laffey and Weldes 2008: 560). Moreover, as Shilliam has shown (2016), the use of the concept of the 'subaltern' does not imply a being whose mind and being is completely dominated by colonial power – indeed, the project of 'decolonising' must in part articulate a 'decolonise-able' subject.

Of course, this is not a new problem. The modern global colonial project in which Western hegemony was historically forged has always had its critics, who, out of necessity, needed to make the intellectual space for moral and political challenges to it through decolonisation. As such, it makes sense to turn to some of the key thinkers involved in this project for inspiration. In doing so I bring together some common preoccupations of a quartet of thinkers involved in the twentieth-century project for African decolonisation in different corners of the globe – Du Bois, Césaire, Fanon and Cabral. Whilst their origins, training and approaches to analysis are diverse, encompassing sociology, literature, psychoanalysis and agrarian political economy, respectively, they nonetheless converged intellectually and politically on the problem of the denial of African subjecthood within European thinking and advocated overlapping responses to the conditions of colonialism.[2]

These overlapping responses contribute to what I call the reconstruction of subjecthood in political analysis. By 'subjecthood' in this context, I mean the property of having one's presence, consciousness and realities engaged in the analysis of the political space. This does not entail in and of itself specific conclusions but is a necessary precursor for analysis of political orders and – more broadly – 'dialogue' about such orders (Sabaratnam 2011: 782). As noted in the previous chapter, whilst the 'local turn' and other arguments have incorporated elements of this, they have often done so in ways which ultimately complement rather than challenge the Eurocentric set-up of the problem. By contrast, articulating the exclusion of target societies as a problem of 'subjecthood' in research gives us a platform for a more systematic rethinking. Whilst the three strategies below overlap philosophically, heuristically separating them helps to map out a pathway for analysis.

Recovering Historical Presence

In anti-colonial thought, it was argued that erasing a society's historical presence was an important part of both colonial strategies of rule and of the Eurocentric political imaginary. Whilst Césaire (2000 [1955]) directs this critique against French colonialism, Cabral (1966) directs it against the Leninist orthodoxies of the European Left, both of which regarded the histories of colonised societies as largely irrelevant both to the political questions of the day and to the history of the world in general. Without a sense of 'African Presence', of past cultures, processes, events and practices, the existential crisis which colonialism had produced could not be discussed, challenged or rejected.[3] Although the histories of Africa presented often took a celebratory form in the context of decolonisation, many thinkers also resisted the temptation to glorify uncritically a precolonial African agency or presence. For example, Césaire wrote about the problem of coming to terms with the painful historical miseries of slavery as an integral part of African history in which Africans participated, even as he articulated the need for a celebration of *Négritude*. The broader point, common to these different orientations, was nonetheless to say that colonised subjects *had histories* in order to challenge the idea that they were blank slates or barbarians waiting to be civilised.

Du Bois, however, also makes the argument that Africa has not only *histories* but *historical significance*, that is, a significance with regard to its contributions to things perceived to be major achievements of human civilisation. In his writings on *The World and Africa: An Inquiry into the Part Which Africa Has Played in World History* (2014 [1947]), he brings together a reading of Africa's contribution to 'antiquity' with his global historical sociological analysis of its place in modernity. This argument is framed this way in order to challenge the racist assumptions common at the time that Africa had no meaningful history or culture and certainly nothing transnational in character. Fanon's analytic of African historicity made more assertive claims about the status of the African masses as an engine of historical change and the redemptive capacity therein for the future of humanity (Fanon 2008 [1954], 1965), although he was more pessimistic about the effects of colonial rule on its contemporary historical presence. Either way, to say that colonised peoples had not only history (i.e. a past of significance) but also *historical significance* was – and in some sense remains – a radical departure from the common assumptions of modern scholarship.

By contrast, it is noteworthy that the majority of scholarly literature on intervention is fundamentally *ahistorical* when it comes to target societies, and this is symptomatic of their Eurocentric historiography.[4] This is either because they do not attend to historical dimensions at all in their analysis, such as in the rationalist analysis of Barnett and Zürcher (2009) or the narrative accounts of Chandler (2000, 2006) and Pugh (2005), or because they are principally focused on the lineages and presence of Western interveners (Duffield 2001, 2007) and/or their ideas (Richmond 2011). In a third variation, historical detail is mentioned simply in passing *en route* to discussing a generic typology of international-local 'friction' (Björkdahl and Höglund 2013).

Therefore, these spaces are analytically framed simply as being interchangeably non-liberal sites of post-war transformations, upon which projects of liberal governance are visited. Due to these sites lacking a historical presence, the analytic effect produced is that of these societies as a 'blank slate'. In this sense, scholars treat the interveners themselves as the primary actors of interest for analysis, with target societies becoming strangely anonymised – in Björkdahl and Höglund's words, cases are the 'diagnostic sites' (2013: 295) for the analysis of political relations.

There are at least two ways in which the failure to articulate target societies as historical entities in their own right has had implications for the analysis of intervention in the scholarship, beyond the general denial of presence. In the first instance, it is largely implied that liberal peacebuilding represents a *novel* form of governance-based liberal social transformation in post-conflict settings. Indeed, in particular cases, such as that of Richmond, it is made to sound as if engagement with the liberal peace represents a novel encounter not only with liberalism but somehow also with modernity in general as opposed to the world of local custom and tradition. This resonates with the colonial projection that African societies were empty spaces historically and politically speaking.

Second is the corollary insinuation that the engagement with liberal intervention is by default therefore an alien and inauthentic form of politics, in which those who adhere to it are understood as either co-opted into its ideology via false consciousness, or engaged in elaborate game playing. Whilst this may be demonstrated to be a useful interpretation in specific instances, to assume it *in advance* of an engagement with political or social history of the actors seems to assume some sort of ahistorical and fundamental ontology of liberal-local difference. We have no sense of the ways in which many societies have been long-inserted into global connections and conditions associated with liberal modernity (Nadarajah and Rampton 2016), which is itself anyway constitutively hybrid (Laffey and Nadarajah 2012). This means we can neither understand the differences between places, nor the contemporary political terms on which they might engage with intervention. Whilst it is a problem across the formerly colonised world, the relative historical length of Portuguese and Spanish colonial rule means that such entanglements are centuries older and in many cases carry their own forms of violence and erasure.

Decolonising the analysis of intervention thus means cultivating an appreciation of the historical presence of target societies and contemplating its significance for the politics of intervention. Histories are of course always contested, and postcolonial historiography has questioned the construction of elite and nationalist accounts of historical presence in the postcolony (Prakash 1994). That said, David Scott (2004) argues that particular kinds of negation demand particular kinds of response. On my specific research question regarding international intervention, an appreciation of historical presence that allows us to evaluate the politics of engagement between international actors and the targets of their reform is appropriate.

For my study of Mozambique in the following chapters, I assume and engage with the historical presence of the state, the peasantry and the politics of anti-corruption, viewing the politics of intervention from this vantage point. This narrative locates and substantiates the territory of present-day Mozambique as being the subject of a series of different projects of modern rule and social organisation, of which the post-war international statebuilding era is a recent iteration. This historical sensibility draws directly on the narratives and context provided by project interviewees, as well as those given by scholarly sources and public histories. This allows an appreciation of questions of continuity and change, of interpretive and practical significance which reframe many of the issues surrounding the politics of intervention. Moreover, an understanding of Mozambique as having a historical presence is necessary to inform a critique which can engage with its peoples as proper 'subjects' of politics.

Engaging Political Consciousness

If the critiques of statebuilding interventions have been content to more or less ignore the historical presence of target societies, they have been equally willing to marginalise the political consciousness of their inhabitants, regarding it as either irrelevant to the question of intervention's legitimacy, or largely tainted or co-opted and thus unable to make authentic or relevant comment upon it. Yet, this also denies subjecthood to target societies; in a meaningful sense one cannot have subjecthood without the implicit assumption of consciousness. In moral philosophy, it is the presence of the capacity for self-reflection – conscience – that renders it possible to discuss action as having moral significance: without this it is difficult to ascribe moral agency as generally understood. Similarly, being able to appreciate a self as a political subject and imputing political meaning to his/her actions must assume a form of political consciousness.

Echoing Fanon's critique of colonial mentality (2008: 3), this overdetermination within the analytic gaze means that the political consciousness of target societies can end up being understood as a form of empty mimicry without its own significance. This construction mirrors the ahistoricism of the analysis, in terms of denying presence and significance to people as proper subjects of politics. For some recent analyses this is the result of a focus on the productive character of liberal discourses of governance, which are thus understood as determining political consciousness (which then does not need to be looked at on its own terms). For others it seems to mark the key political difference between interveners, who are unproblematically 'authentic' bearers of liberal consciousness and people in target societies who are not. Another tendency more broadly avoids interpretive analysis altogether when it comes to target societies, reading politics off manifest behaviour alone.[5]

These habits of ignoring political consciousness in analysis set off several alarms in the context of anti-colonial thought and decolonising struggles. At a general level, the denial of historical presence for colonised societies was interwoven with the idea that the natives' heads were empty and lacking in the proper capacity for politics. This provided a key political rationale for the denial of sovereignty to 'uncivilised' peoples (Gong 1984; McCarthy 2009). This rationale was mirrored in academic terms as well; politics in the colonies was only a matter of if and how these spaces could and should be brought up to levels of European civilisation – matters on which natives could not possibly have as informed views as Europeans. To this extent colonial administration was its own branch of political science (Vitalis 2000), implying its separateness from politics proper.

The decolonising strategies of anti-colonial thinkers addressed this denial of political consciousness directly, but did so from different perspectives and with different objectives. I summarise here two relevant to this study of international intervention. First, engagement with political consciousness was understood to be a necessary decolonising act in its own right; it was a dialectical form of recognition and humanisation to counter the derecognition and dehumanisation effected by colonialism (Césaire 2000). In the context of expressing human and racial equality, a recognition of political consciousness amongst colonised populations established political grounds for rejecting the colonial relationship. Particularly for those forms of scholarship engaged with emancipatory or critical approaches, this should be a reason to think carefully about the implications of systematically excluding the political consciousness of the oppressed in studies of hegemony. This is not to *reduce* critical scholarship to the politics of recognition (Coulthard 2014), or what is sometimes pejoratively called 'identity politics', but to recognise that questions of voice remain an issue when dealing with Eurocentrism in scholarship.

The second purpose – in some senses more important for our analysis – of engaging the political consciousness of the colonised was intellectual and analytic. In this sense it is a clear departure from the politics of recognition. At a general level, one could understand the nature of colonialism differently – and often better – through the ways in which colonised peoples understood and experienced it. We see various versions of this claim worked out in the writings of anti-colonial thinkers. Particularly resonant and influential is Du Bois' conception of 'the veil' (1994 [1902]: 3) which characterised the experience of living as a black subject in the United States: the situation of being simultaneously conscious of the white racist gaze as well as conscious of the power of black subjectivity to see through this. Sometimes referred to as 'double-consciousness', Gilroy (1993: 130) argues that this situation produces a particular and novel kind of political understanding, creativity and prospective space for self-realisation.

Césaire and Fanon had their own accounts of the colonised political subject as politically conscious, and each corresponded to the idea that there was something productive about the colonial condition which gave rise to important differences in the perspectives of coloniser and colonised. For Césaire, this sensibility manifested in his eventual fallout with the French Communist Party (2010 [1956]), which explicitly rejected the possibility of the European Left 'thinking for' the colonised, particularly along lines which did not focus on the specificities of racism. His wider involvement in the Négritude movement celebrating African culture, history and presence proceeded from his belief that they represented a space in which an alternative set of human political attitudes could be cultivated.

For Fanon, colonialism and racism produced specific forms of conflicting and alienating political consciousness (2008 [1954]) which nonetheless also contained within them the dynamic potential for overcoming via struggle and resistance (1965, 1994). Yet, this required, particularly of colonised elites, the relocating of understanding, identification and political consciousness in the experiences, needs and ideas of the colonised masses. It also required a vigilance and reflexivity with regard to the new dispensations of national consciousness. Despite the various difficulties colonised societies would face in seeking it, political subjecthood *per se* was both necessary and achievable in the struggle against colonialism.

Looking at these brief examples together, three pointers emerge for engaging political consciousness as a decolonising strategy. The first is that the roots of political consciousness, and indeed political subjecthood, are *multiple and themselves political* – they derive from the antagonistic social relations of colonialism, the use of culture as a political resource and a conception of the humanity of the colonised. Each of these sources is used as a source for political consciousness, and each gives insight into how colonialism functions. The second is that these are *relational* and not essentialised conceptions of the political subject – coloniser/native and white/black relations are seen as constructed, provisional and there to be overcome by an emancipatory decolonisation. Even in their most 'cultural-ist' form via Négritude, they represent a possibility for a cosmopolitan and humanist future (Wilder 2015). The third is that the 'mundane' or 'everyday' is *political* in its full sense, including individual and group experiences of discrimination, humiliation and frustration.

We have seen in the previous chapter that the study of interventions to date has tended to ignore the political consciousness (and content thereof) of target societies, with a few exceptions. It therefore reproduces a particular hierarchy of knowers and excludes various insights available to it regarding intervention, as well as the possibility of more deeply rethinking the nature of its politics. In this study of Mozambique, I have endeavoured to engage the political consciousness of those targeted by intervention, often by asking interviewees what and how they think about it and looking at this along with other sources of political discourse. Although I am not naïve about the politics of the interview setting, across the wide range of people that I spoke to, there was a very high degree of overlap in their understandings of the nature and functions of intervention which corresponded to both a sense of their own historical presence and of the material conditions produced by the intervention setting. I treat these comments as expressions of political consciousness because they are comments and questions on the nature and distribution of power and the values that underpin it, questions of accountability and the distributive effects of policy. In the substantive analyses of the state, the rural economy and the politics of anti-corruption in this project, my analysis proceeds by taking these views seriously and asking what we learn about the politics of intervention.

Investigating Material Realities

The final decolonising strategy proposed is about engaging the 'material conditions' of societies under intervention. Put simply, this is a 'reality check' on the nature of the problem (Hameiri 2011), which does not assume a correspondence between the stated aims and representations of interveners, and the experience of intervention itself. It is also a counter-narrative to thinking about the political economy of intervention primarily as a function of a specific ideology (e.g. neoliberalism) rather than a concrete system lived by humans in time and space. This element is already present to some extent within the intervention literature and more widely in the literature on the anthropology of aid.[6] But it often stands alone or is bracketed as part of the standard operational failures (inefficiencies, ineffectiveness) of development assistance. Put into interaction with an awareness of historical presence and political consciousness, however, it becomes a powerful basis for critical thinking – *an alternative reality to map and explain*.[7] This resonates with Césaire's method for thinking about colonialism:

> In other words, the essential thing here is to see clearly, to think clearly – that is, dangerously – and to answer clearly the innocent first question: what, fundamentally, is colonization? (2000 [1954]: 32)
>
> They throw facts at my head, statistics, mileages of roads, canals, and railroad tracks.
>
> I am talking about thousands of men sacrificed to the Congo-Océan. I am talking about those who, as I write this, are digging the harbor of Abidjan by hand...
>
> They dazzle me with the tonnage of cotton or cocoa that has been exported, the acreage that has been planted with olive trees or grapevines.
>
> I am talking about natural economies that have been disrupted, harmonious and viable economies adapted to the indigenous population – about food crops destroyed, malnutrition permanently introduced, agricultural development oriented solely toward the benefit of the metropolitan countries; about the looting of products, the looting of raw materials. (2000 [1954]: 43)

Here, Césaire's polemic gestures towards a concrete political economy of colonialism, rooted in situated questions of dispossession and suffering. He is of course well versed in more orthodox Marxist political economy regarding capitalism and imperialism as well, as were most anti-colonial thinkers of the time. However, there was a sense in which simply reading a critique of capitalism off historical materialist categories would not be adequate to the political and intellectual task of decolonisation. Like Cabral and Fanon, he was very clear that a theory and practice of decolonisation was needed which would deal with what we might call the 'phenomenological excess' of colonialism – the ways in which it produced specific patterns of living in the colony and how this translated into ways in which social and political hierarchies were sustained.

Cabral's political economy thinking is also very much of this type, rooted in the concrete effects of colonialism on the peoples of Guinea and the kinds of practice this was built on. His indictments in *Portuguese Colonial Domination*, one of the early liberation struggle pamphlets published in 1960, lists a number of specific complaints against colonialism rooted in dispossession, including the non-ownership of cultivated property, the forced acceptance of low prices, the driving of Africans off more profitable land and crop holdings, the high profits of the colonial companies, the 'native tax' on Africans and the spending of these revenues on Europeans. His comparisons are visually and politically arresting: 'The setting up of each European family costs Angola one million escudos. For an African peasant family to earn that much money, it would have to live for a thousand years and work every year without stopping' (Cabral 1979: 20–21).

This strategy contributes to decolonising analysis in three ways. First, and straightforwardly, it indicates the ways in which colonial discourse misrepresents itself and its developmental or civilising effects. This is significant if colonialism desires to be understood as a substantive project of human betterment and not a hypocritical project of domination and/or exploitation. Second, it exposes the specific ways in which the hierarchy of colonial difference impoverishes and inflicts material suffering on the colonised, again pushing against the idea that colonialism improves and uplifts rather than oppresses. Third, it asks for analysis to problematise the idea that African lives are worth less than those of the European settlers and to begin thinking about political economy on this basis.

With this sensibility in mind, in this study I pursue a specific decolonising analysis of the political economies of intervention as understood and experienced by different groups of people, including public sector workers, media commentators, government officials, donor representatives and farmers, and corroborated with wider studies that attend to these conditions. Within these analyses emerge narratives of its material conditions that are too distinctive to be contained under the more general framework of a global neoliberalism; instead they are evidence of structures emerging from more specific asymmetric relations of hierarchy, income and production within and alongside intervention. These include the political economy of the aid 'industry' as an important productive and relational context for how intervention is practiced and reproduced. However, it is just as important to see this as embedded within wider social relations which pre-exist the post-war interventions and which have not necessarily been transformed by it. It is these patterns which are read through the concept of the coloniality of power in the concluding chapter to the book.

***

To summarise, in order to pursue a decolonising analysis, I argue that we need to begin by assuming and engaging the historical presence, political consciousness and material realities of the targets of intervention. These strategies work against the kinds of erasure that allow political analysis to become largely Eurocentric in its logic and focus, and in doing so they open up intellectual space for an alternative interpretation of the politics of intervention. In the following chapters, I bring together these three decolonising strategies to evaluate the politics of intervention in three contexts in Mozambique – within the central state apparatus, within the rural economy and within the politics of anti-corruption. The final chapter of the book contemplates how intervention can be understood with reference to the findings of these strategies and the question of the coloniality of power in contemporary world order.

However, before this, it is useful to substantiate more clearly the philosophical rationale for how and why decolonising strategies are an appropriate response to the problems of Eurocentrism in *research* – that is, not only in the service of a specific political project but also in the service of a more philosophically robust platform for thinking about global order. In the next section, I do this through working with feminist standpoint theory and its claims for how and why 'situated knowledges' improve our understanding of structures of power – and why this is not just the substitution of one set of biases for another. I address some of the questions it raises through the thinking of black and Third World feminist scholars on the relationship between science and political action. There are significant overlaps between the reconstruction of subjecthood advocated by anti-colonial thinkers and the adoption of situated knowledges by feminist thinkers, and this lineage is noted already in the literature (Laffey and Weldes 2008: 559; Go 2016). Both confront a situation in which political institutions together with standard scholarly approaches normalise the exclusion of specific questions, actors and positions from discussions about politics, even when they form part of these structures in a material sense. Thinking about this as simultaneously a 'scientific' problem as well as a political problem is a necessary step towards better starting points for studying how politics functions.

FEMINIST STANDPOINT, 'OBJECTIVITY' AND EPISTEMIC PRIVILEGE

A basic premise at the centre of standpoint theories is that the knowing subject can never be fully separate from the object of knowledge, thus refusing the idea that most scientific knowledge is naturally 'objective' (i.e. subject-independent) in nature. In this sense, they sit amongst a wide set of critiques of the modern episteme. Rather, scientific knowledge is socially constructed, partial and contains within it a number of biases and blind spots. Thus, claims for the ability of scientific knowledge production practices to transcend particular interests or values by virtue of uniquely superior rational methods should be regarded with suspicion. This generic premise – that knowledge is always 'situated' – is important but not unique to standpoint approaches. What is distinctive – and most controversial – in standpoint theories is the way that this purported *problem* in the nature of modern scientific knowledge is reconstructed as a *resource* for thinking about how to reconstruct sciences 'from below' in the service of subjugated people and groups.

Early feminist standpoint thinkers critiqued the monopolisation of scientific communities by 'masculinist' world views, methods and analytic priorities, which led to the exclusion of women's lives, knowledges and experiences from the purview of scientific knowledge. Dorothy Smith made this argument for the discipline of sociology, which at that point tended to end its analysis of society at the front door of the household in which most women were predominantly embedded. For Smith, this exclusion was emblematic of the institutional complicity of sociology as a discipline with the maintenance of the existing patriarchal social order: 'objective sociology as an authoritative version of how things are [is] done from a position and as part of the practices of ruling in our kind of society' (2004 [1974]: 30).

A key point on which the critique developed was the way in which the notion of scientific 'objectivity' was specifically wielded to reinforce the authority of men and masculine science over the means of knowledge production (Harding et al. 1983, 1991; Haraway 1988). In this sense, it was 'pseudo-objectivity' (Harding 1998) – it had pretensions to be value-free but was in fact presumptively embedded in white, male, bourgeois projects of hegemony. For standpoint theorists, a 'successor science' to this would have to embrace the partial, limited, embodied and situated nature of knowledge practices but radically expand *whose* perspectives and experiences were considered useful, worthy of attention and so on. 'Strong objectivity' as formulated in standpoint theory thus creates a form of *political* triangulation for claims about the world and requires knowers to think about overlaps, resonances and tensions between positions. Science must therefore understand itself as polyphonic, politicised and plural. In this sense, 'strong objectivity' requires reflexivity, humility and openness to multiple accounts of the world (Haraway 1988; Mills 1998 [1988]).

Standpoint theorists, however, also contended that knowledges produced from a position of relative subjugation would be *distinctive* from hegemonic knowledge in various ways. Moreover, many argued that subjugated or subaltern knowledges are not only distinctive but also analytically *privileged* perspectives on how power relations operate in society. Hartsock (2004 [1983]) develops this argument primarily as a feminist reformulation of Marx's method for contemplating the standpoint of the proletariat; others have developed this thought in relation to Hegel's argument about slave consciousness (Harding 2004: 53–54).

The basic argument runs as follows. Under conditions of structured inequality, people occupying dominant and subordinate positions will tend to have different kinds of awareness about their social positions, role and conditions. Although, on the one hand, dominant groups have a greater control over collective narratives and ideologies than subordinated groups, subordinated groups, on the other hand, are nonetheless aware of the limits of these narratives by virtue of their own materially different conditions. In fact, because of the ways in which they are incorporated into hierarchical relations (i.e. of production/reproduction), subordinated groups have an epistemically privileged vantage point when it comes to analysing the nature of social order. Those occupying privileged or ideologically 'unmarked' positions, however, often lack – or indeed suppress – awareness of the various structures and practices which uphold their privileges.

In feminist writing on standpoint theory, the possible sources of feminine epistemic privilege are not singular but multiple. Whilst there is a 'biological' argument made in some feminist writing about the superiority of female cognitive patterns (Mills 1998: 394), most writers make a materialist case for epistemic privilege derived from women's involvement in both productive and reproductive labour. In some cases it is argued that this requires a deeper and more immediate tangible connection with the totality of effort required for human existence (Hartsock 2004 [1983]: 42–43; Ruddick 1980). For others, it derives from occupying a marginal 'outsider-within' position which involves occupying a social space (e.g. as Black women domestic workers and carers) but being invisible or marginalised within it (Collins 1986). Part of the experience of feminine subordination – particularly when racialised for particular kinds of labour – thus involves a great deal of intimacy with privileges that cannot be accessed by women normally. Moreover, it demands expertise in how to *survive* particular systems of subordination.

In each version, there is a case not just for the *distinctiveness* of women's knowledge based on concrete material difference, but the *privilege* of the subordinate position as a place from which to perceive or try to apprehend *more* of the 'totality' of social order in some sense. Hartsock's argument is thus that the sexual division of labour between men and women across time can even be understood as analytically *prior* to class divisions as the major organising principle for society. However, in articulating an intersectional standpoint framing, Mohanty argues that 'within a tightly integrated capitalist system, the particular standpoint of poor indigenous and Third World/South women provides the most inclusive viewing of systemic power' (2003: 232). Thus the case for epistemic privilege is also based on the relationship between the system as a whole and the degree to which specific subjects are marginalised within it.

Returning to our discussion on Eurocentrism in the literature on intervention and the need for decolonising strategies, there are important points to bring in from the discussion on standpoint theory. In the language of Haraway and Harding, the persistence of a Eurocentric framing within the literatures on intervention can be seen as a form of 'pseudo-objectivity' within the present scholarship on intervention. This is because Eurocentric assumptions place limits on how the researcher can think about and engage with the politics of intervention and systematically excludes much of the story and the relevant actors. Interveners themselves are likely to be oblivious to, or indeed suppress, knowledge and understanding which directly challenges their power and privileges. Moving towards 'strong objectivity', however, would require a practice of expanding the pool of knowledges on which a more public, democratic, liberation-oriented science could proceed. In Shilliam's words, an engagement with what he calls the 'non-West' is necessary for 'a more adequate appreciation of the global context of modernity' (2010: 24). The decolonising strategies advanced in this chapter offer a way of engaging and recovering such positions, which would be a way of articulating 'situated knowledges' about intervention and building up a wider account of the phenomenon from there.

Furthermore, when putting decolonising strategies together with standpoint theory, there is a clearer rationale for the argument that these strategies can deliver a 'better' account of social structures than those aligned with the perspectives of interveners (Go 2016). This comes from the argument that the knowledges of subordinated groups can claim epistemic distinctiveness and advantages when it comes to understanding the totality of the system in question. This is intimated by Du Bois in his idea of 'the veil' as a space of 'second sight' for the Negro (1994 [1902]: 3) and in Césaire's emphasis on 'thinking clearly' about colonialism. This is because subordinated groups experience social structures and institutions differently and have a particular familiarity with them, because of under-labouring within them, thinking about how to survive them or struggling against them.

For this research on intervention, my argument is that states or societies targeted by intervention experience them differently than the interveners. Because they have to 'service' the interventions in various ways, they need to think about how to survive them and may also struggle against them. The point is then that the material position of being politically subordinated is *epistemically generative* – that is, gives rise to a different and more holistic way of seeing that particular structure. People on the receiving end of inter-national intervention and statebuilding projects are therefore likely, for the reasons just described, to have a different and *more holistic* way of seeing the system as a whole. This contrasts, for example, with Autesserre's treatment of the situated knowledges of the targets of intervention, which are included but the substance of which (in terms of complaints about colonial or racist forms of behaviour) is quietly ignored.

***

Perhaps unsurprisingly, these alternative approaches to the practice of science have faced objections from different quarters, to which considered and robust responses have been made (Mills 1998 [1998]; Harding 1991). In this section, I summarise some of these challenges relevant to my proposed application of decolonising strategies as well as some responses to them. Given the kinds of scepticism with which such alternative epistemologies are often received in social-scientific communities, it is useful to be clear about the intellectual basis for this way forward.

These challenges come from two different directions. A 'rationalist'/ positivist critique within Marxism suggests that false consciousness oper-ates across the board, including amongst subordinated groups; it thus rejects the possibility of the epistemic privilege within standpoint theory (Mills 1998: 399–402). For the purposes of our study, this resonates somewhat with the argument that 'local' actors are 'co-opted' into the interventionary frame-work, which might lead us to be sceptical of rooting analysis in the perspec-tives of subordinate groups. Developing this line of argument, we might argue that the very nature of political hegemony requires it to generate consent and acceptance amongst the subjects over whom it wishes to rule, meaning those subjects are likely to internalise many of the perspectives of dominant groups.

As a wholesale rejection of standpoint analysis, however, this does not seem plausible. When one examines the concrete histories of self-awareness and lib-eration struggles by oppressed groups, they often do *demonstrate empirically these capacities for distinctive analysis and action*. The uprisings of the enslaved and the Maroons in the Haitian Revolution are an increasingly well-understood example of this capacity (Shilliam 2008, 2017; Buck-Morss 2009). One should of course be interested in the specific historical conditions under which, for exam-ple, the conditions of enslavement gave rise to the Haitian revolution, or women around the world were granted voting rights. One might also offer criticisms of the limited ideologies or world views under which forms of liberation were achieved (white imperialist feminisms or patriarchal nationalisms, for example).

However, it is difficult to sustain seriously, in the face of the historical record, a thorough-going *rejection* of all of these kinds of self-awareness as equivalent forms of false consciousness to their historical opponents in analytic terms. It is not the case that both the slavers and the enslaved had opposing, but equally valid and equally misguided, views of slavery as a system. Similarly, I would not expect targets of international intervention to labour under grand illusions that were significantly disparate from their experiences of it over a long period of time, particularly with public and private spaces in which critical discussion can take place. As will be seen in Mozambique, although there is a desire for more such spaces and less party-politicisation of them, they exist in many settings and have been used to generate critical awareness of multiple kinds.

From the other direction, post-structuralist critiques have questioned the utility of holding to broad unifying labels such as 'woman' in feminist methods, because this does not foreground the fluidity of gendered categories, the multiplicity of positions and experiences held by different women and risks reductionism or even biological essentialism.[8] Moreover, claiming epistemic privilege and a progressive normative framework is seen to attempt to resurrect the old Enlightenment violences of Truth and Reason as a means to discipline dialogue. It may also reinforce hegemonic patterns of binary thinking and cement the control of particular kinds of women or feminists (usually cisgendered, straight, white, able-bodied, middle-class) over the political agenda. For many years, and perhaps especially in the present, this question has been at the heart of feminist discussions about the nature of political thought, analysis and action.

Thinking through this critique in the context of this study, this would mean problematising the labelled position of 'Mozambique' as a place from which to speak, because (i) it does not foreground the fluidity of positions within the country, (ii) it essentialises 'national consciousness' in a binaristic way and (iii) it may well privilege official/elite/masculine actors relative to non-state/non-elite/feminine voices and positions in discussing intervention because of their relative ability to appropriate the label. It may also seek to discipline narratives through their correspondence or not to a particular set of 'truth claims'. Given the general investment of decolonising strategies in combating exclusionary tendencies, these are important issues to address.

In response, standpoint theory emphasises a kind of perspectival realism (Mohanty 1993; Go 2016: 162–166) which is compatible with the post-positivist claim that knowledge is theory-dependent. On the first point, Collins' (1997) response to Hekman (1997) is that structured oppression is not experienced by individuals incommensurably but by groups, and these structures are durable over time and space, even though there is fluidity within them. As such, for standpoint theory one cannot simply substitute the 'individual' for the 'group' as a locus of analysis; indeed, denying an epistemological basis for talking about group experiences works to deny the possibility of talking about structured oppression at all (1997: 377). In fact, the concerns of the second and third critiques of representation require that other structured oppressions have their own group-based realities which can be identified, albeit not under a singular mode or voice of analysis. In terms of thinking about our 'decolonising strategies', the purpose is precisely to affirm a collective subject that has been previously negated, denied or ignored but which can share truths about the nature of oppression.

Relatedly, the purposive, pragmatic defences of 'science' and 'truth' put forth by Haraway (1988) and Harding (1991, 2008) suggest that oppositional logics can generate understandings of oppression, even if they are also subject to reasoned disagreements about the nature of that oppression. Looking at the strategies of Third World feminists, Chela Sandoval (2004 [1991]) argues that the retention of an oppositional logic has been necessary in order to preserve political space for their critique. Yet, this is only one amongst many methods of political organisation and 'tactical subjectivity' (2004: 203) available to Third World feminists, who engage with it as one mode of struggle and survival. In this vein, many are sanguine about the possibility of using 'the master's tools to dismantle the master's house' (Hutchings 2003: 148).

In thinking about the implications of studying intervention, the point is then that in this particular context of inquiry (i.e. the construction of Eurocentric knowledge about intervention), it is useful and legitimate to contemplate a framing which engages tactically and practically with a political context in which the 'beneficiaries' of intervention as 'states'/'countries'/'societies' are recognised groups with experienced realities and claims to make, even if analysis is not limited to those frames. There is thus a warrant for talking about 'Mozambique's' experience of intervention in analysis – being 'Mozambican' has a specific meaning in this context. It does not imply, as was well understood by anti-colonial thinkers, that nationalism and national identity is an end in itself, but rather a space of experience and intellectual tool to achieve a degree of liberation.

This clarification also speaks to the third critique of representation mentioned above – namely, the overtaking of a broad collective identity by narrower and sectional articulations thereof within the feminist movement. This is a well-known area of discussion amongst black and Third World feminists (Mohanty 1988; Sandoval 2004), as well as queer theorists (Butler 1990), many of whom have argued that there is a tendency amongst white and liberal feminists to over-homogenise women's experiences, assume a representational role for all 'women' and call for 'unity' in order to enforce homogeneity within the feminist movement. In this sense, the position of white and liberal feminists may be analogous to the role of national, metropolitan elites in talking about 'Mozambique's' experience of aid in discussions on intervention.

On this point, humility, reflexivity and accountability are important but only partial responses. The spirit of triangulating perspectives to generate 'strong objectivity' infuses the research design of this study, and to this extent I have endeavoured to seek out engagement outside and beyond metropolitan-based elites in Mozambique, with the various caveats about my own positions and how access to non-elite respondents can be pursued. These involve the use of new labels and positions, for example '*camponeses* / peasant farmers', which themselves are infused with hierarchies of privilege, access and representation which are also classed, politicised, gendered and – to a lesser extent – racialised. It is nonetheless a limitation of this study that proportionately, within the material studied for this project, much of it is drawn from 'elite' sources.

Yet, in the context of this inquiry, even a limited study such as this has the potential to generate new questions, categories and analyses for our understanding of the world. To return to Collins' point, however, the acceptance of shared realities is a necessary starting point for any discussion of structured oppression, even if such structures themselves contain other forms of structured oppressions or erasure. This project focuses on the relations of intervener and targets as a strategic response to situations in which the latter has been made absent from the analysis.

CONCLUSION TO PART I

The traditions of critical thinking now present in IR offer much promise as resources for thinking about world politics differently. However, they have their blind spots, inherited and reproduced in specific ways of thinking about the world. The previous chapter demonstrated the general absence of the subjecthood of target societies in much research on intervention as part of this intellectual terrain and located this tendency within the philosophical co-ordinates of Eurocentrism. In this chapter I have elaborated some decolonising strategies for challenging that in a methodologically reasoned and sustained way. The strategies identify and challenge particular absences – historical, political and material – and elaborate these strategies as consonant with feminist philosophical arguments for standpoint approaches.

IR as a discipline would benefit greatly from the much wider application of these strategies if it wants to take forward its aim of understanding how world politics works. In this sense, these decolonising strategies open up spaces for challenging the habituated provincialism of IR and its narration of world affairs. The following three chapters use these strategies for thinking about different aspects of the politics of intervention and statebuilding as they have evolved over the last two decades – the nature of the state, the rural political economy and the politics of anti-corruption. These different approaches generate different interpretive frameworks for intervention and explanations for why it fails, rooted in experiences of the social and political hierarchy between interveners and targets. The final chapter asks how we can think differently about intervention when we use these decolonising strategies and a critical mindset to analyse the problem.

NOTES

1. These principles are also described in Sabaratnam (2011).

2. They are nonetheless distinctive thinkers in their own right and each has inspired a rich scholarly literature. For a selection of key works see Reed (1997), Wilder (2015), Wynter (2001), Gordon (1995), Chabal (1983) and McCulloch (1983).

3. This refers to the journal set up by Alouine Diop in 1947, *Présence Africaine,* with which Léopold Senghor was also associated.

4. Notable exceptions here are Heathershaw (2009, 2010), Goodhand (2005), Autesserre (2010); Rutazibwa (2014).

5. Mac Ginty's (2010) qualifier is that scholars may lack the 'antennae' for such analysis.

6. For example, in Pouligny (2006), Autesserre (2010) and Smirl (2015), as well as Mosse (2005).

7. An important exception to this lacuna is Turner and Shweiki's volume on de-development in Palestinian political economy (2014), which explores the concrete effects of aid within the context of colonial relations with Israel in the vein proposed here.

8. See Hekman (1997) and responses.

Part II

RETHINKING INTERVENTION

Chapter Four

The State Under Intervention

When you are poor, you have to accept the game.

—Civil servant, Nampula Province

Help which does not help is not help.

—Provincial official, Nampula Province

On my first visit to Mozambique, I found myself in the office of the country director of one of the largest international NGOs, which had projects across various sectors. He had been in post for a few months and had very little Portuguese. On the walls of the office was a large map of the country. 'So', he said, 'can you tell me a bit about what the war was about? And who exactly are Renamo?'

Stories of this kind – where interveners know very little about their host countries – are not uncommon in Aidland.[1] Put differently, in the intervention relationship, the weight of history and memory sits heavily on one party but often hardly at all on the other. Interveners tend to rotate through posts quickly, particularly when working for national development agencies. Furthermore, as Autesserre (2014) demonstrates, their roles do not depend on having knowledge of the national context. By contrast, for nationals of the country – plus some of those from abroad who have chosen and succeeded in making their homes there – the intervention relationship is one which is soaked in historical experiences and common reference points, struggles, upsets, failed reforms, scandals, triumphs, lost energies and slow, ground-out time.

This chapter works through an account of the state under intervention in Mozambique, through deploying the decolonising strategies developed in the previous chapter. That is to say that the account of the state is rooted in a sense of its historical presence, the political consciousness of the people who inhabit it and an account of their material realities. Thinking about the state in this way highlights a number of particular dynamics within international intervention that are often occluded by other accounts. Specifically, explained by the targets of intervention, these elements are the consequence of structures of aid dependency, on the one hand, and what is called donor *protagonismo*, on the other. These two heuristics of intervention are key elements to how the targets of intervention explain its ongoing dynamics. These dynamics include the unbuilding of the state through fragmentation of its infrastructures, the draining of its human resources, the waste of efforts on capacity-building activities and the experiences of public services as better but fundamentally unreliable. Whilst these dynamics are well known and well understood by many of those involved in intervention, they are understood by its targets as persisting because of the structures of dependency and *protagonismo* in which they are embedded. The chapter first locates the post-war statebuilding project historically and describes the context of intervention, before examining its key dynamics in terms of the functioning of the state. It finally turns to the question of how the targets of intervention make sense of its effects on the state and its functionaries.

BUILDING THE POSTCOLONIAL STATE

To make sense of intervention after the war, it is important to locate our understanding in the postcolonial statebuilding project launched after independence. Mozambique achieved independence from Portugal in 1975, following a long guerrilla campaign in the north of the country, international pressure and a coup inside Portugal from an army tired of fighting colonial wars. Frelimo – the Front for the Liberation of Mozambique, and the leading organised political force – assumed power and embarked upon an energetic programme of African socialist statebuilding. In part, it had little choice – many of the productive industries, farms and various offices held by Portuguese settlers had been abruptly abandoned, meaning that nationalisation was the only way to get them going again. Yet, it also cohered with the ideological vision for a modernising, egalitarian, state-led society inherent in the Marxist-Leninist commitments of the vanguardist party leadership.

To give a sense of the public services and statebuilding challenges, at independence, it is estimated that there were only eighty trained doctors in a country of ten million people, and the population was more than 95 per cent illiterate. In this context, the first international assistance for statebuilding in independent Mozambique came from other states in the Eastern bloc that were willing to supply medical staff, teachers, equipment and advisers to the new government and included *cooperantes* – volunteers, often young Westerners attracted by the promise of creating a socialist society – who were also used to fill administrative and technical roles, particularly in the ministries. Young Mozambicans with any education at all – often from middle-class and/or white settler families – found themselves with senior roles in government and industry very quickly. In addition, those who demonstrated their worth through participation in the independence struggle for Frelimo were entrusted with major offices. Collectively they oversaw attempts to exponentially expand education and health services, agricultural production, infrastructure development and other public goods. This statebuilding project was underpinned by Frelimo's commitment to the cultivation of a 'New Man' in the wake of colonialism – a scientifically minded, egalitarian, collectivist citizen who cast off both imperialism and sorcery in building the future.

This fragile and ambitious experiment in African revolutionary statebuilding was almost immediately put under severe internal and external pressure through the 1980s. The inexperienced new order found it difficult to make things work, and various enterprises collapsed under their own weight. This was in spite of – and sometimes because of –international assistance, from both Eastern and Western bloc donors, in some productive sectors such as sugar and public services such as health. Affairs were also severely disrupted by the beginning of a long and bloody war. Funded by white regimes in Rhodesia and South Africa, Renamo (Mozambique National Resistance) began a campaign of violent destabilisation and sabotage, targeting schools, hospitals and roads, drawing in part on resentment created by Frelimo's state-building and collectivisation programme. Up to a million people are thought to have died as a result of the war, with around three million internally and externally displaced. This conflict absorbed huge amounts of government attention and funds on its own terms. Coupled with tied loans, the drying up of Soviet support, the losses from the state industries and expansion of public services through the country, Mozambique found itself in a major debt crisis by the mid-1980s. Moreover, these crises had severely disrupted even the most basic systems of food production and people were starving – many to death – all over the country.

A large Structural Adjustment Programme (PRE in Portuguese) was agreed to with the Bretton Woods institutions and implemented in 1987, in which debt relief and development aid were traded for a floating currency, large cuts in public spending, taxation reform and a comprehensive privatisation programme. The levels of official international aid from the West virtually doubled between 1986 and 1987 (De Renzio et al. 2007: 4). At its peak, in 1988, foreign aid constituted 81.2 per cent of GDP. In Frelimo's Fifth Congress, held in 1989, this recalibration of relations with the West was articulated as the necessary price for the pursuit of its historic mission – indeed, the

price of survival. By this time it was also apparent that neither side in the
war could win in military terms, and by 1990 a ceasefire and formal peace
talks had begun in Rome under the auspices of a Catholic lay organisation.
Mozambique's socialist experiment appeared to be over.

INTERNATIONAL INTERVENTION IN
MOZAMBIQUE AFTER THE WAR

In the early 1990s, alongside the peace deal (1992), the UN-supervised
electoral process (1992–4), the disarmament, demobilisation and rehabilitation (DDR) programmes and the integration of some Renamo fighters into
the national army, there was a massive influx of emergency relief aid as
well as development aid. As people went back to their homes, development
aid became the major vector of international intervention in the state. After
substantial complaints that organisations were functioning in parallel with
the state, this development aid emphasised explicitly its orientation towards
national capacity-building. Within government, ministries began to function
more fully and sought to co-ordinate aid flows, projects and programmes
alongside their own activities more clearly. Despite serious and prolonged
contestation over the 1999 elections by Renamo, there was no attempt by
the donors to encourage a recount even in light of a recognition of electoral
irregularities.

The presence of international organisations was highly visible throughout
the country and in government in this period, with a very mixed influence
in different areas. However, a specific and widely publicised episode was
influential in shaping attitudes towards the Western donors in Mozambique
and beyond. This was the World Bank's intervention into the cashew industry in the 1990s. Mozambique had been the world's leading cashew exporter
at independence and by 1980 had developed fourteen processing plants,
supported by an export tariff which prevented the export of raw cashew
nuts. The World Bank, on the advice of external consultants, insisted on
the removal of this tariff through the withholding of earlier-promised state
loans, which resulted in the collapse of the cashew-processing industries
and the loss of thousands of jobs in those zones. Following unrest, a new
system of export tariffs was quietly reintroduced, but the episode weighed
on relations between the government and the donors as well as public
perceptions of it.

Co-operation with international donors on virtually all areas of public
life, however, deepened through the end of the 1990s and into the 2000s
and was given renewed vigour through three major and related developments. One was the Highly Indebted Poor Country initiative (HIPC),

which provided a major tranche of debt relief to Mozambique co-ordinated by the international financial institutions (IFIs). This required the production of a Poverty Reduction Strategy Paper (PRSP),[2] which created softer liberalisation targets and planning processes in various sectors and a process for overseeing their achievement. The second was the institutionalisation of the Millennium Development Goals and the commitment from wealthy countries to increase aid flows to 0.7 per cent of GDP in order to help meet those goals. The third was the aid harmonisation and effectiveness agenda, embodied in the Paris Declaration on Aid Effectiveness in 2005, which underscored the principles of 'national ownership' of spending priorities and delivery through general budget support, sector-wide planning and 'mutual accountability' between donors and recipients (now both referred to as 'partners'). Within Mozambique all three of these developments impacted the size, nature and governance of international aid, particularly in sectors seen as driving human development such as health and education. From 2003 to 2008 official aid from Organisation for Economic Co-operation and Development (OECD) countries increased by about US$500 million, an increase of around 40 per cent (Cunguara and Hanlon 2010).

Yet, the relationship was also underpinned by a more vocal concern with corruption on the part of the donors, instigated by the murders in 2000 of a journalist and bank director who were investigating corruption in the privatisation of the Bank of Mozambique. Pressure in the form of threats of withholding aid was put on the government, which was perceived as acting slowly to find and catch the killers. The president's own son, Nyimpine Chissano, was accused of having ordered the killing of the journalist but, surprisingly, died shortly after his indictment. Since then, various public projects have been marked by allegations of corruption or malfeasance.

The combination of increased attention to anti-corruption measures and the national ownership agenda led to a large public sector reform programme, supported by international co-operation, focusing mostly on the production of a new financial management system to be used across government. This was intended to support the channelling of international funds through the state budget. Yet, since 2010, donors have been increasingly retreating from direct contributions to the state budget and financing alternative providers of public services. The discovery of oil and gas prospects in Mozambique has changed the nature of state finances, as has a recent decision to incur non-concessional public debt for the purchase of fishing industrial equipment and other state expenses (Wirz et al. 2016). Whilst the donor footprint continues to be substantial in Mozambique, particularly in specific areas of public service delivery, increasingly the state is seen to be taking the lead on policy issues and donors are feeling rather less influential.

WHAT KIND OF STATE HAS BEEN BUILT?

Intervention constantly positions itself in relation to its imagined future, but not its lived past or present. In its future, there is greater capacity, greater service delivery, greater ownership and greater legitimacy. Reports and strategies for the next donor programme rarely refer to – let alone evaluate – the programme that preceded it or those running alongside it. Each is born innocently into a future-oriented conversation where its primary reference points are itself, contemporary global targets, and the new people whom it will uplift. Scholars, too, evaluate interventions in relation to this promised future and ideal-typical co-ordinates, thinking constantly about how it could be improved *next time* and, in innovating, thus transcend its present limits.

Accordingly, to even talk about the histories of intervention is to interrupt a narrative which wants to focus on a promised future. To think about these pasts and presents from the experiences of those targeted by interventions is a further interruption. The following sections are narratives about the present and recent past of the state in Mozambique as constituted in a time of international intervention and statebuilding. They show that the effects of intervention – designed to *build* the state – have contributed to its fragmentation. As argued in chapter 6, this problematises the view of intervention as promoting 'good governance' in the global South.

Fragmentation of State Infrastructure

One of the principal effects of intervention in the institutions of the state has been a fragmentation and dissipation of efforts in specific sectors despite concerted attempts to control these effects. The experiences of the health sector – one of the largest recipients of international assistance in Mozambique and central to the historic project of postcolonial and post-war statebuilding – are illustrative of such dynamics. Whilst other sectors will have their own experiences, one would expect a sector perceived as an urgent priority and which was well funded to be amongst the leading beneficiaries of assistance. However, in contrast to the expectations generated by statebuilding discourse, Mozambique's health sector has seen a contested but now effectively institutionalised incoherence in how it functions at the level of government and on the ground. This is in spite of the widely held understanding that uncoordinated aid presents specific problems for its intended beneficiaries. A former senior ministry of health official evaluated the historic relationship as follows:

> The relationships between Mozambicans and their foreign counterparts has varied a lot. In pharmaceuticals, drugs, we can distinguish over different periods. Just after Independence, we had enough money, and didn't need any foreign

help – the health sector was narrow. As the system increased, the need increased and the health sector became broader. This coincided with the civil war, around 81–82, when we couldn't afford to import drugs. In 83–84, we started to get some health aid in kind. Even the socialist countries used to pledge *things on a list defined by us* [emphasis added], and donations were on this basis. It was also typical for larger INGOs to decide the needs of Mozambique. They sent huge shipments, but no one knew what they were, what was coming and the management of the system was not easy.

In 85/86, limitations were found with the system, *it could be seen that aid was hurting not helping* [emphasis added]. The tentative co-ordination started then, because of drugs. In 86/87, there were also signs of a changing relationship with the Bretton Woods institutions. They were discussing the possibility of financial aid, which helped pave the way. This started with the establishment of a co-ordination mission; this was twice a year – we met with the major partners, the government, the banks etc. There was a meeting to discuss the mechanisms for moving from in-kind to financial aid. This was way before SWAp [Sector Wide Action plans]. The decision-making process moved from bilateral, in-kind aid to multilateral and financial aid. The relationships changed from one-one to one-many, to discuss activities. The results of this were impressive – it was making the best possible use of the money.[3]

The 1980s, in this reading, represent a time when there was some government control over health services, somewhat undercut by INGO activities but later better co-ordinated. Despite a seemingly progressive movement towards co-ordination, however, the last fifteen years has seen the emergence of huge internationally controlled, disease-specific – what are called 'vertical' – funds at the global level that has specifically worked against such attempts. The same official tracked the activity since the 2000s:

With AIDS, the move to support grew especially from 2000, 2002 – funds grew a lot in 2004, 2006 – the tendency to support has increased. The picture changed a lot, because the initial support came from the World Bank. Let me go back. Along with this process, MISAU [the ministry of health] had project support from the World Bank, but in terms of management, they attempted to integrate them, even though they were separate. With the attempt to grow the Ministry of Health and CNCS [National AIDS Council], there was the same project approach. Also, PEPFAR [US President's Emergency Plan for AIDS Relief] appeared, and the Global Fund [for AIDS, TB and malaria]; which also adopt a project approach. These couldn't be integrated into PROSAUDE [Common Funding and Planning for the Health Sector] because of the reporting back requirements. Now it is a parallel mechanism. Also, in theory it is aligned, but in practice it is separate. PEPFAR had the major impact: Firstly, because USG money does not flow to other governments, and second, because the implementation of government plans goes through NGOs, usually US NGOs, if you look at the COPs [Codes of Practice]. In the Common Fund, you are looking at how decisions are made. With PEPFAR, the declaration is made, that it is to support the ministry's plan, but by mandate they cannot transfer money: they are using money through NGOs. There are several tiers of decision-making: at the diplomatic level, *these are usually unilateral decisions* [emphasis added], although they are supposed to be based on the relationship between NGOs and the government.[4]

By the mid-2000s, the minister of health had taken to referring to himself as the 'minister of projects'.[5] Most of all, the layered and fragmented planning system absorbed large amounts of time and energy for those concerned, manifesting itself often in back-to-back meetings with different partners in the ministry. In one extreme case in a different sector, it was reported that a single NGO had sent six different delegations from different programmes to the same ministry on the same day.[6] Another former public health official reports:

When I was there, we did a National Plan. Then the World Bank came with a map, and wanted a plan for the map. Three months later, Clinton [the Clinton Foundation] arrived, and asked for another plan. In the next three months, the Global Fund came, and they needed another plan – I said, 'No, sorry', and then PEPFAR – I refused. I said, 'Sorry, we cannot'. We need to do a big national plan and then use it to develop some things.[7]

The scale of fragmentation is also pronounced. The Mozambican Ministry of Planning and Development has undertaken a series of evaluations of the Paris Declaration in recent years in an effort to record levels of national ownership and mutual accountability in international co-operation. Its data on the health sector reflects the rollback from the use of national systems in recent years towards project finance and vertical funds. The latter not only have their own time frames, reporting requirements and budgeting arrangements, but also require input in terms of time and resources from the government in terms of approving and monitoring the activity.

Figure 4.1 shows the respective proportions of the health budget spent through different channels. *Contra* the aspirations of the Paris Declaration, in which national systems are presented as the best channels for aid effectiveness and ownership, the trend in the Mozambican health sector has been in the opposite direction for some years, mostly due to the effects of the large vertical funds (PEPFAR, Global Fund, Clinton Foundation). These now account for well over 60 per cent of the money spent in the health sector in Mozambique. By contrast, the proportion directed by the government by its own funds or common funds is less than 40 per cent. There was an attempt to bring the Global Fund for AIDS, TB and Malaria into the common funding system, but this had to be abandoned, as the finance flows were too unpredictable and untimely, producing serious problems (Government of Mozambique

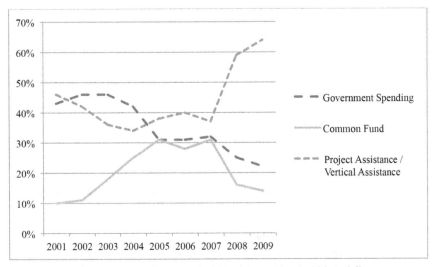

Figure 4.1. Percentage of Mozambique's Health Sector Budget by Aid Modality, 2001–2009. *Source*: Government of Mozambique (2010: 53).

2010: 55). Perhaps ironically, even the attempt to co-ordinate such fragmentation has itself produced three different co-ordination mechanisms (54).

In addition, many bilateral donors, including the United Kingdom, Norway and Finland, have abandoned the common fund arrangements and are contracting directly with subcontractors for health provision in Mozambique. In the case of the United Kingdom, previously one of the central donors to the common fund, one of the factors cited has been the *progressive decrease in influence it has been able to have on policy through common funding arrangements*.[8] Instead, the post-2010 approach to aid in the United Kingdom has emphasised upward accountability to itself and is testing 'payment-by-results'.[9] Rather than the progressive institutionalisation of a functioning state-led system in the sector delivering public goods, the effect of intervention over the last ten years appears to be working in the opposite direction, despite the creation of the relevant financial and planning systems at the state level, and despite widespread recognition that lack of co-ordination is a key contributor to aid ineffectiveness.

Disappearance of Human Resources

> The Minister of Health says, 'I was walking in the hospital, and one of my doctors says to me, "do you have a secretary's position?" I ask "Do you need one?", and the doctor says "I would like to apply"'.[10]
> —Former minister, Government of Mozambique

This is an old joke told in the health sector in Mozambique. Unsurprisingly, one of the major consequences of the fragmentation of the state is the constant loss of qualified staff – the 'brain drain' to international organisations and/or the private sector, and often other professions altogether. This is either through full absorption or through public sector staff taking unpaid leave to work for these organisations, at all levels from the ministry downwards. Intervention has generated both 'push' and 'pull' dynamics for staff to leave the public sector, despite the critical importance of staff retention to capacity-building, institution-building and service delivery.

> The motivation that drives people to go to work in NGO? Are the conditions themselves. When I say working conditions I mean the salary. For example, we have a doctor in NGO who has there 100,000 meticais or 85,000 meticais, receives it in dollars, and converting gives 85,000 meticais or 100 000 meticals. And there is an employee in the system, the same course, the same category, who is receiving only 8,000 meticais, with the various costs that the person has. These are reasons that make people not think twice or three times to leave the health sector. Unfortunately. It is our reality and we don't have the means to fix this.[11]
>
> —Pharmacist-turned-hired-driver, Nampula Province

This reading is corroborated by Pavignani and Durão (1999), both former senior health sector workers in Mozambique, who argue that the inability to pay salaries is one of the most critical weaknesses of the Mozambican health system. In terms of the 'push' factors, the structural adjustment policies adopted in Mozambique have substantially depressed public sector wages in both absolute and relative terms (Marshall 1990; Pfeiffer 2003; Pfeiffer and Chapman 2015). Indeed, large numbers of publicly trained doctors have also left the country altogether in search of better salaries, with one estimate putting this rate at 75 per cent of all doctors for Mozambique in the years 1999–2001.[12]

Another less well-understood 'push' factor is the political effects of attempts by politicians to clamp down on time wasted on international initiatives inside the ministry, which had also provided financial and professional opportunities for those working there. Former civil servants and doctors who had walked away from their government jobs to jobs in European development agencies and donor programmes argued, implicitly in their defence, that they were ultimately doing the same jobs but with another organisation, with better conditions.[13] Yet, it was also clear that the dynamics of international co-operation produced alienation in multiple directions inside the government.

Such dynamics of alienation, opportunities and fragmentation are also highlighted in Pfeiffer's study (2003) of the impact of international co-operation in the health sector in central Mozambique. He argues that due to the tightening of state health budgets, and the willingness of external projects to set up broad systems of incentives, including per diem payments and other benefits for participation well in excess of standard salaries, the provincial health system had become significantly fragmented and incoherent, whilst remaining understaffed. This fragmentation led to public servants spending a high volume of their time managing co-operation programmes and projects or being at workshops, rather than managing the affairs of the health service (for those who stayed within it). For health professionals who managed to leave and join an NGO, however, Pfeiffer calculates that the value of the salary and benefits could be up to twenty times what could be earned within the state, meaning that even this short-term work could easily become more attractive than long-term work with job security in the state.

The critical problems in human resources within the health system are well understood and have been highlighted for a long period of time. In light of the crisis provoked by the loss of staff, the Government of Mozambique initiated agreement on the 'Kaya Kwanga' commitments in 2000. These promised to align donor remuneration in the sector with the state, and particularly not hire qualified people out of the ministry, in which the retention of capacity was critical. However, these commitments were not observed and the practice continues to be widespread. At the time of one of my visits in 2009, eight senior people were hired simultaneously out of the Ministry of Health by a single donor to run a new health programme.[14] Indeed, the former Mozambican national director of human resources for the Ministry of Health, who has over twenty-five years' experience and has published precisely on the problems of the 'brain drain', now works as country director for ICAP (International Center for AIDS Care and Treatment Program), an international NGO and research organisation, which is a large and generously funded vertical provider of HIV/AIDS services. As explained by a senior civil servant, the persistent turnover of staff and the loss of experience was a serious problem for the government:

> This is very negative – you have to explain things again. Those who know the reality, the instruments – lots is not written. When a new person comes, it is difficult. *They think there has been no change* [emphasis added] ... There is a tendency for much change – even new secretaries. The know-how disappears ... This is an illness – a cancer.[15]

Capacity-Building?

Almost every concept of international statebuilding is oriented around the idea that a key part of the challenge for the fragile state is to increase and strengthen the institutional capacity to administer and deliver public services, by having internationals train nationals. A recent World Bank Institute report noted that US$20 billion is spent by donors annually on 'capacity building' in 'developing countries' (Otoo et al. 2009: 1). Yet the same report argues that 'the results of efforts to develop capacity have persistently fallen short of expectations' and cites previous findings from the institution, which say:

> Most efforts at capacity development remain fragmented, making it difficult to capture cross-sectoral influences and to draw general conclusions. Many capacity development activities are not founded on rigorous needs assessments and do not include appropriate sequencing of measures aimed at institutional or organizational change and individual skill building. (Otoo et al. 2009: 1)

Within Mozambique, amongst the targets of capacity-building, these problems are very well understood, and they produced scepticism both within the government and outside it towards these activities. In particular, concerns are articulated over the large imbalances between 'training' and actually carrying out any work. A recent minister of health tapped into this scepticism when he effectively banned ministry officials from participating in various donor seminars and workshops (*capacitação*: workshop) as part of a broader crackdown on corruption in the sector. The student who told me this argued that these workshops did not have any benefit but 'they were just happening to pay the teachers, to pay the organisers, to buy some water, but they didn't add anything'.[16] More broadly, they have been understood to be time- and resource-intensive, poorly implemented and often inappropriate. This is complemented by scepticism towards much of the 'technical assistance' in ministries – international advisers seconded by development agencies – which has, with noted exceptions, not been experienced as particularly helpful.

This sensibility resonated with my own interpretation of the five-day health leadership training workshop in Maputo funded by the United States Agency for International Development (USAID) described in the Introduction to this book. In discussing the impact of aid, the leader of a governance-focused NGO also problematised the value of capacity-building workshops more generally, arguing:

> So of course, when they do the evaluations of these projects and programmes, everyone is satisfied ... Everyone talks about doing 'capacitação' – but what have they done in the last 20–30 years? People that come to deliver this are not appropriate – can you imagine taking a Mozambican to the UK to teach them? This is not capacity ... *And still people lack the resources to implement the programmes* [emphasis added].[17]

'Capacity-building' had become not just focused on the government ministries, but has been adopted more widely as a model for how to spread development knowledge in civil society organisations and communities. Here it was also understood as not simply ineffective but resource-absorbing. A former civil servant and state enterprise manager argued:

> A lot of money goes to training. I know it's important but it depends on how you do it, and I found that most of the training is not effective, and you go around and you see and it's not working. I think that could be analysed why, 'cause very often people, they want to do training, but either you do it well, and it may cost a lot of money, or you do it small, something small, but donors want numbers – they want to reach millions of people.
>
> So you train a full province? You haven't trained anybody … I was asking people, 'You are asking two people from the community? They don't read or write, they badly speak Portuguese, and you train them for a week on a subject, and you want them to go back and train other people? You are mad! It can't happen, you can't ask that from people. It's not what they have to do, they *can't* do it. You [the consultant] studied that, I don't know how many years, you receive a lot of dollars for that, but in the community they didn't study, they don't anything, and they don't receive for doing that. So you give them their work; *your work you give to them* [emphasis added], and they are not paid so you can't do that'.
>
> … So these numbers, these things of the numbers, and I think a lot of money was thrown out unfortunately. Because you have this programme, for three years you have to train 1,000 people on I don't know what. Okay, you bring all of them to the classes and what, what, what in three years? Most of these trainings have to change your mentality … you don't change in three years. You finish that training, it's finished, and no one will look at that again. You don't go back to work and look at it again, so all the money went in what? Salaries for trainers.[18]

The Ministry of Agriculture in particular channelled much of its statebuilding funds (PROAGRI I and PROAGRI II) into 'capacity-building' in the ministry at the central level. Whether or not the specific training was useful, by the end of the process, most of the staff had been hired outside the ministry, meaning that for the most part any positive effects of capacity-building were not left within the state.

***

The faulty assumptions at the root of most capacity-building practices have been well understood by academic approaches to public administration since the 1990s (see Grindle and Hilderbrand 1995) and acknowledged by international policy centres in the years thereafter (OECD 2006; Otoo et al. 2009). These studies suggest that skills transfer via training – the primary modality of conducting capacity-building in practice – may not actually better enable individuals and organisations to accomplish their objectives. The experience of those subject to such programmes repeatedly and from many different providers corroborates and extends this sensibility. This leads to the suspicion not only that they may not be helpful, but that their primary objective may be the work-making character of the training itself. Yet, this is the main form in which 'international statebuilding' exists – through the provision of capacity-building exercises, the limitations of which both recipients and funders are quite aware.

Citizen Experiences of Public Services under Intervention

To the extent that the state is conceived as an organisation whose role is to deliver public goods, the effects of intervention culminate in a deeply mixed set of experiences. On the one hand, using the end of the war as a baseline, public services, particularly in terms of education and health, are much more visible and functional in Mozambique than previously, and it is widely understood that this would not have been possible without international assistance. In particular, the physical infrastructure for these services – schools, hospitals and clinics – is much more visible and donors who have contributed to such are gratefully acknowledged within this physical infrastructure through badges and plaques. Indicators such as pupil enrolment and maternal mortality[19] demonstrate the expansion that has taken place over the last thirty years from a very low level, particular for primary services. Amongst my interlocutors across Mozambique there was also general agreement that health and education services had certainly improved.

On the other hand, in interrogating the experience at ground level in healthcare, it became clear that service delivery is itself also strongly conditioned by different dynamics that speak to the presence of intervention. As discussed, one is the absence of qualified health workers, particularly in rural areas but also in urban ones. In response, the government has trained a large number of technicians to carry out a range of basic to medium-level functions that ideally fully trained doctors or nurses would conduct. Yet, these workers are also subject to the unstable conditions produced by depressed wages and the system of incentives to work for other employers. As a result, health services are very irregularly staffed, meaning that patients also are reluctant to waste their own time and resources attending clinics.[20] These can be particularly high investments for each patient given the difficulties of transport and infrastructure. Moreover, and less frequently admitted in donor/policy studies, there are widespread reports of problems of health workers soliciting bribes to supplement their wages for appropriate levels of care or medication.[21]

In addition, the frequent rigidity of project- and disease-specific healthcare interventions – whilst important – also strongly skews services and their provision in certain ways. A former civil servant noted that the weight of

AIDS-specific funding was seriously out of proportion with that in the rest of the sector, meaning that the wider systems needed to support patients did not function. As a result, the patients still died from preventable causes:

> The AIDS clinics were very good, but the rest of the health, no. But you go to the AIDS clinic when you're not sick, when you are still not sick. When you are very sick you go to the hospital, but your hospital doesn't receive all that money so people die in the hospital, but they die of AIDS. Because of AIDS they die of pneumonia or whatever, but it's because of AIDS, but there they are not looked after conveniently because the hospital did not receive the money but the AIDS structure did.[22]

Health workers and activists working with HIV/AIDS patients, who were enabled by international intervention through vertical funds, also discussed the rigidity of the support given, which, for example, proscribed the giving of a small food basket as an incentive to come to the clinic, which would also allow patients to eat better to allow the medication to work.[23] Clearly, the vertical funding was central to their work but not flexible enough for people working in the health centres to maximise the effectiveness of the resource. Depending on the channel, others were more successful in appropriating funds for diverse purposes not linked to the provision of care itself. International HIV/AIDS money ended up supporting theatre groups and leisure facilities that advertised themselves as raising awareness of the disease, even when this link was admittedly oblique. This money is all recorded as having been spent on health services.

Yet, for citizens not integrated into the public health system, and perhaps some who are, there is evidence of significant distrust in terms of how it functions. In Nampula Province, for example, from 1998 to 2001 it was widely believed in some of the coastal areas that the state and NGOs were trying to introduce cholera into the water supply, in order to poison the population. This led to vigorous uprisings, including the burning of houses and public protests, which subsequently led to many arrests and one death. Although the confusion may have stemmed from the similarity in words for 'cholera' and 'chlorine', the extent to which it ignited public anger suggested a serious and wide set of grievances and mistrust towards the state and the international NGOs working in the area. Indeed, there were widespread fears and rumours that public health workers, such as those vaccinating children, had come to kill them (Serra 2002: 27–28).

Serra (2002) argues that various forms of structural disconnection had emerged, leaving the public feeling both disempowered and distrustful of the seemingly arrogant and distant parties who claimed to be working for their benefit but often did little of value or solicited kickbacks in exchange for attendance. Rather than long-standing superstition being the cause of this, there was no history of such uprisings in Nampula. Serra argues that that the more immediate causes were the context of local elections which had increased political tensions in the district, plus new intervention programmes by an NGO. Whilst such open conflagrations are relatively rare responses to public service failures within Mozambique, they seem inexplicable without postulating that there is a broader suspicion towards the state and the seemingly eccentric priorities of public health staff – both national and international – in terms of how they operate. Indeed, such suspicion can be understood as a fully rational response to the experiences of the state by the citizens.

***

Whilst there is no single account of the many different facets of the state over the last twenty years, international intervention in statebuilding in Mozambique has clearly been a dynamic and visible presence. However, these dynamics have to a large extent been a force for fragmentation and instability rather than consolidation and coherence. As can be seen, these kinds of fragmentation and instability characterise its uppermost levels as well as delivery on the ground. In the next section, I explore how these dynamics are interpreted and reflected upon by its targets.

THINKING LIKE A TARGET OF
INTERNATIONAL INTERVENTION

The dynamics of fragmentation and the disappearance of capacity described in the previous section are drawn largely from a close study, specifically of the health sector, but resonate with experiences in other sectors in Mozambique. In an open letter to Hu Jintao in 2007, Mozambican journalist Marcelo Mosse argued:

> We are poor but we are not blind, and we like ourselves! Because of this, over the years, we have criticized the Western donors for the negative aspects that their 'cooperation' implied; we criticized the destruction of the cashew industry; the re-indebtedness of 'technical assistance'; the excessively rigorous controls on public spending; the (disastrous) imposed privatisations; inappropriate technologies; the so-called 'tied aid' (which China promotes today); the project implementation units; the disempowerment of the state, the inefficient and unending capacity building etc. ...
>
> A lot of money, credit and donations have been spent on these processes. We could be better, of course. We're not. However, the country has changed its face, we have more schools, hospitals, better communications, roads, maturing institutions, etc. In short, despite the negative aspects of such cooperation, there are many visible gains. Yet despite this, we remain dependent.[24]

Indeed, there is good reason to believe that these dynamics are more broadly recognisable to the targets of intervention across a wide range of contexts over the last thirty years or so, where many of them have become clichés.[25] In the global policy-directed literature, they are glossed as problems of the 'effectiveness' of intervention, which might be remedied through the sharing of best practices, the establishment of better relations and the propagation of new concepts such as 'capacity development'.

The targets of aid in Mozambique, however, articulate these primarily as political questions located in the materially unequal and asymmetric relations between interveners and target societies, within which struggles for coherence, sovereignty and presence take place, alongside a quest for resources. This sense of the reality of intervention is a widespread and common sensibility that both *describes* and *interprets* its dynamics. Significantly, this consciousness is widespread and came up repeatedly throughout the research:

We on the ground are making noise – we shout, we shout – but, well, we have to conform because we are a poor African country and we have to live like this. And we will continue living like this. In this way, some will continue to get poorer, and others will be much richer, and in reality what can you do? The only secret is to study, isn't it, to see if you can escape, work in the NGO and have more money.[26]

—Former health worker

Of course, they [the partners] have a big influence. We are a very poor country, where 50–60% of the budget is paid for by them. It's indisputable.[27]

—Newspaper editor

The partners at the moment have a heavy weight in Mozambique. This derives from the financial aid to the budget of the state – I don't know exactly how much it is. But it gives them a great power, from those that give a small amount, to a big amount – it gives them disproportionate weight. But Mozambique, during many years Mozambique has lived off this. It has created a certain dependency – like a drug addict, it does not think whether it can live without the drug or with less of the drug.[28]

—Director of national NGO

The differences are very old – this is an old story, that the NGO has all the money and the government has nothing.[29]

—Former agricultural technician-turned-social enterprise worker

The collective understanding of this inequality that emerges is of the reality of aid dependency: a permanent, weighty, debilitating impoverishment in which individuals, groups and the government must function and do what they can. In more measured language, this sensibility of deep asymmetry has even made it into government documents:

> *The relationship between donor and aid recipient is unequal by nature,* and ignoring this fact runs the risk of threatening the creation of structures that are not used to their fullest potential or as understood by the Paris Declaration [on aid harmonisation]. Ultimately, the issues of ownership and responsibility, and *even other seemingly more technical aspects of the Paris Declaration, depend on real change in mentality and a real change in the nature of the relationship* [emphasis added]. (Government of Mozambique 2010: 36)

This structural and material asymmetry between donor and recipient – the new language of 'partnership' notwithstanding – is fundamental to explaining how and why interventions work as they do, and how the targets of intervention deal with it. When Mozambique accepted a large programme of aid restructuring from the IFIs in the late 1980s, many were acutely conscious of the loss of its control over economic policy and key sectors.[30] Yusuf Adam, a prominent intellectual within Frelimo, noted that the combination of war, destabilisation, emergency and the debt crisis were all contributing factors in forcing the decision to seek more external aid (Adam 1990). The national elite and wider public clearly understood themselves to be in a position of dire emergency. International aid, together with its trappings, was seen to be the only way to alleviate the problems in the short term (Ratilal 1990). Yet, it is now viewed as a time when much had to be accepted, sometimes humiliatingly:

> We were in a situation where a partner would come, want to help, but didn't trust us – they said we had many 'attributes'. So it was difficult – we had to learn to swallow frogs – we had to accept this humiliation. We needed to weigh the results of this position. If you are very weak, if you stick to a point, it's difficult to move. They used to say 'it's up to you, we can always go next door'. But our schools were destroyed, the infrastructure was destroyed, so people would be in a lower situation, or we had to accept it. Some of the partners did this to put us under their control. But we accepted to change and internally reform in a lot of cases. But where we could, we managed to get some ownership, even having the resources from elsewhere. Our cohesion and sense of dignity was always in place – we needed to balance the gains. But with our own ideas. Instead of trying to find justification for why things were like this, we said, let's just concentrate on our own problems. If the problem is coming from the US or Europe, it's their problem. It is a waste of time to work on something we can't influence. Let's concentrate on what we have to do.
>
> —Former government minister[31]

Since this time, the government and other actors have been engaged in a careful and demanding negotiation of the asymmetric relationship with the donors, both trading compliance for aid flows and attempting to take control where possible of the policy agenda.[32] This has involved, on the one hand, engaging with the fragmented co-operation infrastructure in ways which retain lower levels of control over sectoral planning. For example, sources within government and donors are of the view that although the Poverty Reduction Strategy Papers were elaborated and worked on extensively with the multilateral donors, and were important to win debt relief and funding, they may actually have a relatively limited impact on the public policy finally enacted.[33]

On the other hand, it has involved a fairly serious attempt by the government to mobilise the aid harmonisation agenda to establish forms of co-ordination and mutual accountability that underscore its prerogative to shape policy and action:

> Paris [i.e. the Paris Declaration on Aid Effectiveness] says that they have to follow our plan.... Some partners want to influence what is going to be there in 2010, but we said we'll wait until after the election [in 2009]. If it happens that we want one indicator, and they others ... we know that some will be problematic to comply. The Government is sometimes constrained. But there is always a strong dialogue, discussing this. At times they force the Government to implement something.[34]
>
> —Senior civil servant

Mozambican economist Carlos Castel-Branco describes Mozambique as existing under conditions of *multidimensional aid dependency* (2008), which is structural and historical in nature, and which heavily constrains an attempt to establish meaningful 'ownership' over policy as well as the range of choices available, particularly over the meaning of 'development'. He notes that some analyses present this as a rational-choice issue, where external donors are paid more attention than parliament, because it is they who pay. This would be consistent, for example, with the model developed by Barnett and Zürcher (2009) regarding intervention. They argue that peacebuilding creates weak statehood because of the different goals and strategies of the different actors. Specifically, national elites are said to 'covet the resources offered by peacebuilders because they can be useful for maintaining their power' (2009: 24).

Understood from below, however, Barnett and Zürcher's highly reductive and perniciously caricatured way of approaching the dynamics fails to capture the long and frustrated history of efforts to build a functioning state and deliver public services that has underpinned much of the activity over the last thirty years. These efforts have, however, been riven with the fragmentation of policies, institutions, efforts and resources repeatedly and over time. Certainly, the weight of the donors comes with the resources that they bring, but resources are not sought by the government only out of greed or covetousness. If one looks closely at the dynamics over time from the point of view of the target, one sees aid approached in a more cautious and reflexive manner, and in light of a political project, albeit one which is increasingly in question. In this light, the relations are often rather more self-consciously transactional, their effects limited and their institutionalisation more fragile. In Castel-Branco's characterisation, multidimensional aid dependency is first and foremost a historical situation which conditions the imperatives of governments in a very particular way.

Other developments have lessened perceived dependence on the Western or 'traditional' donors, which demonstrate the fragility of the intervention relationship and the significance of financial dependency as its basis. One is the emergence of 'new' donors from the global South who are willing, for various reasons, to do business differently. Whilst this is not perceived as having uniformly good effects – particularly where natural resource governance is concerned – it is understood to proceed on a much more respectful and egalitarian set of political co-ordinates. For example, the Government of Mozambique's evaluation of aid effectiveness has this to say about Brazil:

> Brazil does not impose conditions on its support to the Government of Mozambique over and above the basic reporting requirements. In particular, Brazil does not impose political constraints, and suggests that political development and the development of citizenship should be a goal to achieve and not a precondition for help, as these evolve once a certain social and economic development is achieved, *arising as a result of historical and social process and not due to pressure from a donor* [emphasis added]. (Government of Mozambique 2010: 29).

In practice, the experience of working with 'new' donors has itself been more contested (Alden et al. 2014), and various public protests have been launched against the agricultural and extractive projects proposed. That said, the perception is still that they are prepared to co-operate in a much less rigid way than the Western donors, who looked, by contrast, outdated. As a former minister argued:

> One of the reasons is the rise of other sources of finance, for example, India – access is much easier … We will go for that with or without World Bank permission. The Bank has to reform itself – that will give some fresh air.[35]

This ease and flexibility is directly contrasted with the practices of the Global Fund for AIDS, TB and Malaria. The Global Fund is a private, independent Swiss foundation which channels large amounts of official and multilateral aid, and which is understood as having had a significant short-term impact but at very significant transaction costs for the government and the nature of the health system (Government of Mozambique 2010: 29).

The government has also engaged for many years in 'donor shopping'. This involves looking around for a donor willing to support projects or policies that others will not, or to step in when others pull out. The director of a national civil society fund also noted that this tended to make attempts at co-ordinated conditionality much weaker: 'anyway, if one goes, there will be another to fill their place – Swiss, American, Dutch – there is no common agenda. It is all an industry of competition'.[36]

Amongst numerous examples of this over recent years is the launching of a national development bank for private sector credit, which the government were unable to persuade the large multilateral donors to underwrite.[37] However, in the following years, they signed accords with the Portuguese government[38] to do precisely this for US$500 million. This move importantly undercut an apparent plank of neoliberal economic orthodoxy which sought to liberalise the financial industry and allow the market to set interest rates and repayment schedules. Instead, it offers subsidised interest rates for longer-term investments.[39]

Breaking and/or subverting relations of dependency has been a clear objective in the ways in which co-operation has been conducted in recent years in Mozambique. Increasing its sources of international aid, leveraging its natural resources and trying to create a fiscal base have been all responses to the dysfunctional dynamics of statebuilding under conditions of pronounced structural aid dependence.

Within the international aid industry, however, the dynamics described throughout the chapter are extremely well known and well understood. They are also well understood by the targets of aid. The question is not then, 'why does this happen?' The question must be, in part, 'why does this still happen?', given what is known, and indeed what is spent on both intervention and the contemplation of its modes of functioning.

The way in which it was explained to me by various respondents was in terms of a constant desire for *protagonismo* on the part of the Western donors, which would always undercut attempts at co-ordination and control on the part of Mozambique, and indeed other attempts to make aid more 'effective'. There is no suitable English translation for this word; it is a dramatic metaphor relating to who is the central character of a storyline (i.e. the protagonist). On one occasion a specific organisation was characterised as *gringa*, and sometimes 'having a big ego'.[40] But the word used more than any others was *protagonismo*. This pervaded the way in which agreements were made, the demands for innovation and claims to be innovative, an insistence on conducting their own new studies in a field despite the existence of the same or very similar ones from other organisations or from the government itself, the desire for meetings to happen always at the ministerial level rather than with lower-level officials, the detailed and time-consuming reporting and sign-off requirements, even for small organisations and small amounts of resource, and the demand for results to be immediately reported and available.

As a heuristic, I suggest, the sense of donor *protagonismo* is central to explaining and understanding the realities of intervention, in a way which goes beyond the existing literatures, beyond an account of bureaucratic imperatives and institutional frameworks, inefficiencies and hybridisation. At its root it is an idea which theorises the relations of subjects within a system as political entities, and in terms of their human, flawed, desires for recognition, a performance of mastery, a need for attention. The interveners are seen to exert *protagonismo* not because it fulfils a functional need necessarily, but in some sense – at least to the recipients – it represents a statement about the presence and the importance of the intervener.

Such a concept helps to make sense of the backlash against the traditional donors. As argued by a civil society worker in Nampula:

> For its part, the government says, 'If you influenced the way we got here, it is because you paid. You made a contribution to our budget. And we didn't have the capacity or the voice. Today we have the capacity to finance it, because we can gather more funds and taxes. We want to speak for ourselves, we want to think for ourselves, we want to have our own ideas'.[41]

In this reading, to think about *protagonismo* is to think about how relations are conducted – whose ideas and demands are on the table, who gets to call the meetings, whose priorities are listened to and by whom. It is distinct from dependency, particularly insofar as some donors, particularly the Nordic ones, were often commended for being better able to cede the political agenda to the targets of aid despite high levels of funding. *Protagonismo* is instead about a political relation in which intervention is understood as a kind of space for actualising the identities of specific interveners and their world views, rather than working towards a common agenda set by the government or community. In the final chapter of this book, we will reflect further on the significance of *protagonismo* and more broadly what it means to think with and see with the targets of intervention and what it means to 'decolonise' our thinking.

***

The realities of statebuilding under international intervention in Mozambique are complex, but the story may be a familiar one to those acquainted with aid environments. Through applying our decolonising approach to reading the state, however, we can see an interpretation of failure as not grounded simply in bad policy or bad implementation, but structurally embedded into political relations of aid dependency and of *protagonismo*. In order to see these dynamics, the analytic perspective needs to be embedded in a sense of the historical presence, political consciousness and material realities of those targeted by intervention. This is crucial for an understanding of intervention as a phenomenon and a contemplation of its political significance.

As this chapter has shown, not only is there a significant gap between its stated intentions and realities, but the targets of intervention also have clear ways of making sense of this gap which speaks acutely to its dynamics. In the next chapter, we will extend this discussion by looking at how target communities amongst the rural poor have experienced and navigated intervention. By working with the decolonising strategies set out in chapter 3, a reading of intervention in the agricultural sector reveals not only similar dynamics of state fragmentation to those in the health sector but also wider historical structures of political indifference towards the conditions of the peasantry on the part of both interveners and the state.

NOTES

1. A term coined by Apthorpe (2005) and reworked by Autesserre (2014).

2. Abbreviated as PARP (Plano de Acção para Redução da Pobreza) or PARPA (Plano de Acção para Redução da Pobreza Absoluta) in Portuguese.

3. Interview with former Ministry of Health official, Maputo, 17 June 2009.

4. Ibid.

5. Interview with European donor agency health official, 16 June 2009.

6. Interview with former public servant, Maputo, 12 August 2014.

7. Interview with former Ministry of Health official, 22 June 2009.

8. Interview with Department for International Development (DfID) official, Maputo, 14 July 2014.

9. DfID (2013).

10. Interview with vice minister of Planning and Development, Maputo, 19 August 2009.

11. Interview with pharmacist working as a driver, Nampula, 24 July 2014.

12. BBC News (2008), Africa 'being drained of doctors', http://news.bbc.co.uk/1/hi/health/7178978.stm. Accessed 2 September 2011.

13. Interview with doctor, US-government-sponsored HIV/AIDS program, Nampula, 6 August 2009; interview with agricultural specialist, European development agency, Maputo, 20 August 2009.

14. Interview with head of co-operation, European Development Agency, 22 August 2011.

15. Interview with public official, Maputo, 24 August 2009.

16. Diary notes, 22 June 2009.

17. Interview with director of national civil society organisation, 17 August 2009.

18. Interview with former public servant, Maputo, 12 August 2014.

19. Although the figures on maternal mortality have been produced from raw data which does not necessarily show the same drop. See WHO (2015) figures: http://www.who.int/gho/maternal_health/countries/moz.pdf.

20. See also ODI (2014) report: https://www.odi.org/sites/odi.org.uk/files/odiassets/ publications-opinion-files/9073.pdf.

21. Interview with youth hostel worker, Maputo, 10 June 2009.

22. Interview with former public servant, Maputo, 12 August 2014.

23. Interview with community healthcare worker, Beira, 9 July 2009.

24. M. Mosse (2007), Carta Aberta a Hu Jintao, *Diário de um sociólogo*, http:// oficinadesociologia.blogspot.com/2007/02/carta-aberta-de-marcelo-mosse-ao.html. Accessed 30 August 2011.

25. See accounts in Chambers (1995), Mosse (2005) and Autesserre (2014), amongst others.

26. Interview with pharmacist/driver, Nampula, 24 July 2014.

27. Interview with newspaper editor, Beira, 6 July 2009.

28. Interview with head of national civil society organisation, Maputo, 21 August 2009.

29. Interview with agricultural specialist, Nampula, 13 August 2009.

30. See Munslow (1990).

31. Interview with vice minister of Planning and Development, Maputo, 11 July 2008.

32. This reading of the behaviour is at odds with that offered by Castel-Branco (2007), who argues that the government has little interest in true ownership of the policy agenda, in part because the space for alternatives is in a fundamental sense lacking. I am sympathetic to his argument but suggest that at some times, in some ministries and sectors, the attempt to take control has been genuine and had some limited effects. It is, however, strongly constrained by the factors that Castel-Branco identifies and which I report here.

33. Interview with technical consultant, Ministry of Planning and Development, Maputo, 19 August 2009.

34. Interview with public servant, Maputo, 24 August 2009.

35. Interview with vice minister of Planning and Development, Maputo, 11 July 2008.

36. Interview with director of national civil society organisation, Maputo, 17 August 2009.

37. Interview with consultant, Ministry of Planning and Development, Maputo, 19 August 2009.

38. Negrão (2009), 'Mozambique, Portugal, agree to set up $500m investment bank', http://www.netnewspublisher.com/mozambique-portugal-agree-to-setup-500m-investment-bank/. Accessed 17 October 2009.

39. It has recently been revealed that the government has secretly undertaken US$2 billion of public debt at non-concessional rates, against the macroeconomic policies of the international institutions. The politics of indebtedness and finance are extremely interesting at this juncture but cannot be explored for reasons of space.

40. Interview with civil society leader, Nampula, 23 July 2014.

41. Interview with civil society leader, Nampula, 30 July 2014.

Chapter Five

Intervention and the Peasantry

We're only asking for help. That you help us, because each time they call a meeting, they ask us the same things and don't help us with anything, they don't do anything we ask – they only know how to call us for meetings. What's more, because people are in the field, and they say, 'Mama, run, you have to go there' ... It's just for them to meet with us and when we tell our problems they are not attended to ... You're the third group this year ... people just talk and go away and don't do anything. They just come to watch us make noise.[1]

—Women farmers, Anchilo

The women farmers who had been gathered to speak at our request were the immediate targets of a US-funded local development project which ticked many boxes in terms of current trends in international aid. The project focused on the creation of a private sector entity which would become sustainable by starting businesses to supply grain milling services to households as well as offering some public outreach services. The women themselves said that they benefited greatly from the mill and that having to perform this task manually previously took a long time. Yet, they were also palpably frustrated with the wider context in which NGOs came and went, opportunities were given to some and not others, projects which had started had stopped suddenly, their own communities lacked some of the promised infrastructure and they 'continued sitting there'. Why could they not come to Maputo, or to London, to talk about their problems? Why were there no resources to do the things that had been promised?

In this chapter I open up the political space occupied by these women, who are the disappointed 'beneficiaries' of international intervention. In doing so, I apply the decolonising strategies articulated in chapter 3 to the sphere of agricultural development. Its argument is that when looking at intervention in the agricultural sector through an embeddedness in the historical presence, political consciousness and material realities of the peasantry, such interventions come into view as largely indifferent, irresponsible or fragile. This is in contrast to the narrative of intervention as innovative and transformative – a narrative which animates both interveners' own optimistic accounts and those which are more critical of intervention models. By thinking about intervention through and with the perspectives of the peasantry, including the accounts of farmers themselves, their representatives and allies, we can better understand what it means for intervention to be 'non-transformational' in terms of its presence and put this in the context of historical patterns of both 'development' and 'de-development' within rural production. We can also better understand what alternatives have been put forward by peasant movements and why.

The chapter begins by summarising the political context in which intervention in the agricultural sector takes place, through underlining the symbolic importance of the peasantry to both the state and donors. It then contrasts this with the experiences of intervention from the point of view of peasant farmers, who underline the ways in which it has been largely non-transformative and fragile in terms of improving conditions of production. The character of intervention on the ground is then contextualised in terms of the political activity at the level of the state and donors in agricultural co-operation, which is rooted in contested policies and processes for developing agricultural production, with some shared commitment to an export-oriented strategy rooted in international and domestic large-scale investments. These visions for agricultural production are contrasted with those of the peasant movements in Mozambique, which have, with the material help of interveners and the global peasant movement, created some political force around laws to protect peasant land tenure and emphasise food production for domestic consumption. The political logic of these campaigns is situated in a long view of the peasantry and the historical attempts to govern them and their production strategies, which have been both externally oriented and subject to forms of external sabotage. The chapter concludes with a discussion of how frustrations amongst the peasantry are rooted in the presently visible possibilities for uplift around them, to which they are perpetually refused access.

***

It is worth clarifying the use of the term 'peasant' in the analysis below. The majority of people in Mozambique – around 70 per cent – are defined academically and administratively as belonging to the 'rural' population, 99 per cent of whom are defined as being agricultural 'smallholders' in state surveys.[2] The term 'peasants' [*camponeses*] is used here as an emic term, which many of those who largely live and work for themselves off the land use to describe themselves. This is not to suggest, however, a single type of lifestyle, pattern of production or political positionality. Indeed, rural social orders in Mozambique, as everywhere, contain their own heterogeneous hierarchies of status, respect, wealth, class and access to public goods. Moreover, many of those who live within them have, through both choice and necessity, had to diversify their forms of income and production to make ends meet, resulting in a large amount of labour migration both near and far for 'non-farm' activities.

The identity of the *camponés* is, however, one which has endured and been reproduced in the contemporary era, albeit in changing ways. Although any substantive account of social and political life in Mozambique must account for the fate of the *camponeses*/peasantry, for a decolonising interpretation of the political significance of intervention, the *camponés* must figure centrally in the analysis. The research for this chapter largely focuses on Nampula Province, 2,000 km from the capital and the most populous province in the country, in which 85 per cent of the population live to some degree off the land (Ministry of Agriculture and Food Security 2014).

THE POLITICAL SIGNIFICANCE OF THE PEASANTRY

The state of the peasantry is of considerable political importance to many parties within Mozambique. For the ruling party, Frelimo, it is part of what ideologically stitches together the struggle for independence from colonialism and the former liberators' ongoing dominance of the political arena. The country's 1975 constitution says that Frelimo freed 'the land' as well as 'the man' from colonialism, and the country's post-independence flag contains, deliberately, a hoe, a Kalashnikov and a book. Certainly at the level of the symbolic order, Mozambique has understood itself to be a land of liberated peasants. Even during the liberalisation reforms of the late 1980s and early 1990s, Mozambique's 1990 constitution declared that 'agriculture is the basis of national development' and, against some external pressure at the time and afterwards, that all land is the property of the state and all Mozambicans are free to make use of the land as their fundamental right.

For international interveners, ostensible efforts to help the peasantry helped rehabilitate their image as supportive and developmental after the crises precipitated by economic liberalisation in the 1990s. The major political 'success' of international co-operation was the ubiquitously cited statistic showing a fall in absolute poverty in Mozambique from 69 per cent to 54 per cent from 1996–7 to 2003–4 (INE 1999, 2004). This was revealed to be the result of increased consumption and production in rural areas – that is, amongst the peasants (Fox et al. 2005). This number became emblematic of the potential of Poverty Reduction Strategy Papers (PRSPs) as a 'post-Washington consensus' policy instrument to a much wider global audience. This played a part in re-legitimising the role of the IFIs, UN organisations and European/North American donors both within sub-Saharan Africa and further afield after criticisms were levelled at the impact of development policy.[3] Poverty reduction figured strongly as an orienting objective of international aid in the articulation of the Millennium Development Goals and the 'Make Poverty History' campaign of the 2000s. The successes in absolute poverty reduction in Mozambique allowed the government to enjoy the status of a 'donor darling', receiving funds from across the international aid infrastructure.

Consequently, the moves towards providing aid as direct budget support to the government and away from project aid were closely tied to the perceptions of a successful implementation of the PRSP (PARPA in Portuguese), summarised by the statistical drop in absolute poverty. Furthermore, the statistics on absolute poverty reduction have been an increasingly important part of the government's own electoral manifesto in recent years as its post-independence and post-war popularity has started to wane.[4] Constituting the majority of the 'absolutely poor', the fate of the peasantry in Mozambique is thus intimately tied to the political standing of the post-war aid architecture and government 'performance' as a whole. Given the significance of the rural poor to conceptions and symbols of state legitimacy, international development and economic progress, it is unsurprising that since the end of the war, both the state and international interveners have developed a large array of programmes, projects and plans for the uplift of the peasant and for rural development costing hundreds of millions of dollars.

However, these headlines have not always lent themselves to a wider appreciation of how Mozambican peasants over time have experienced and understood their realities, which is fundamental to decolonising the analysis, as argued in chapter 3. As the following section shows, in contrast with the outward celebration of rural poverty reduction in Mozambique, the experience of supposed beneficiaries is one of limited assistance, repeatedly deflated expectations, unrewarded efforts and a sense of being blocked from more meaningful transformative activity by the systems in place. And yet, due to the dearth of other options and the need for resources, many peasant farmers have sought to glean what they can from international co-operation projects which continue to promise better incomes and better futures, and which even occasionally deliver a more concrete opportunity in terms of direct employment. Such opportunities are, however, both rare and unpredictable, and auxiliary to the objectives of the interventions themselves.

PEASANT EXPERIENCES OF INTERVENTION IN THE AGRICULTURAL SECTOR

There is a lot of effort [by us] – peace always brings this. The peasant tries to increase his areas of production thanks to the peace and freedom that he has. But, for example, at the level of agriculture, we do not have technical assistance. We don't have the seeds to sow on time – for example we're now in August, and we will begin the campaign [of sowing] in September, October. The peasant doesn't know what to expect from the government. He'll make the effort and we try to produce our own seeds, conserve our own seeds. We plant them, what we can. *He's doing it, but we've been waiting for twenty years* [emphasis added]. To improve rural extension, more help for the peasants, more seeds – there's a lot of good things that could help increase production. But today very few of these things – except for what we can fight for in organised groups – are there. But a peasant on his own doesn't have them or wait for them … These are the things that worry us.[5]

—Peasant farmer provincial representatives

The war in Mozambique between the government and Renamo forces from the late 1970s to 1990 for the most part took its worst toll in rural areas. Whilst cities were better fortified, poorly supplied forces swept through the countryside and villages looting for food, mining fields, destroying infrastructure, killing and raping villagers and forcibly enlisting fighters (Magaia 1988; Nordstrom 1998). Apart from the direct deaths and displacements caused by the war, the early 1980s became known also as the *tempo de fome* or time of hunger because of the disruption of basic food production, with many dying of starvation. Farmers often could not sow, plant or cultivate new areas of land because movement was both difficult and dangerous. Sometimes people would venture back to their fields and homes in the daytime, having slept in the bush to avoid night attacks, to see what could be retrieved. Without other means of subsistence, this was the only way to avoid starvation, even though it entailed a high risk of death. As schools, hospitals and other government buildings were subject to targeting by the rebels, many were abandoned or shut. Roads were also occupied by military forces, meaning that they were avoided by civilians and subject to much damage.

The advent of a ceasefire in 1990 and a peace deal in 1992 paved the way home for many of the rural populations who had been displaced internally or across the border as refugees. In discussing to what extent their lives had been transformed since the end of the war, many simply contrasted war with peace; peace meant freedom to sleep in their own houses, cultivate land, that their children could go to school and study, that they could go to the market without fear of being attacked.[6] Others noted that the roads were better and that there were more health centres around. More broadly, it meant something like a future: 'People can dream, work towards their dreams, even if they cannot realise them. But they are now dreaming, "we can do this"'.[7] Whereas the war had meant 'not knowing if you were going to wake up in the morning',[8] peace had allowed something like a normal life to emerge.

Although many thousands of fighters were offered relatively generous demobilisation packages by interveners (Alden 2002), much of the repatriation after the war was 'spontaneous' in the sense of being undirected and to some extent unsupported although overseen by the UN. Much emergency food aid was present in the immediate aftermath of the war but phased out within a few years as farming resumed and emergency funds were withdrawn. However, alongside the food aid, an 'explosion' of international NGOs (Mosca 2011: 370) arrived and began working directly with the population on various aspects of rural development, often as the implementing arm for Western governments (Duffield 2007: chapter 4). Projects included the rehabilitation of rural roads, the provision of seeds and hoes for farming, the creation of water posts and support for land title registrations. Interventions also emphasised the creation of associations for various purposes – crop marketing, savings and credit networks, public awareness about health and so on. Evaluations of projects claim their impact through the large membership of these associations, numbering in the hundreds and thousands.

Promoting Productivity

Specifically within the agricultural sector, a large proportion of international NGO interventions have had the objective of improving production and productivity. Many of these interventions have involved delivering training packages in conservation agriculture, linear sowing and intercropping, which are techniques designed to increase yield in small plots. After the immediate post-war period and the demobilisation packages, the trend has been for interventions not to supply seeds or equipment. Instead, a few people are selected from different groups to be trained, and they are then encouraged to train people in their own communities to spread the knowledge. They are also encouraged to form associations in order to self-organise and receive training and other interventions, as well as to sell collectively. Most of the *camponeses* with whom I spoke, all of whom were members of associations, had received several training sessions, and some reported that they had managed to increase their yield as a result. Others spoke of the range of things that they had learned:

> NGOs helped here by showing us how to sow, how to sell, how to conserve when we have some left over, how it is when we are hungry; we didn't know

that cashew trees should be sprayed but now we know that when they are sprayed they are very fine. These are the things they taught us – how to form associations was also the work of NGOs.

—Farmers' forum, Ituculo-Nicane

Indeed, these packages are significant for the fact that their implementation does not require any new equipment or ongoing support to peasant farmers to implement them. In this sense, according to interveners, they are understood to be 'sustainable' because they do not create 'dependency'.

Yet, as was repeatedly pointed out by respondents, this also means that actual productivity gains and income growth made as a result of NGO interventions are also very limited. Instead, there was a sense that these interventions had reached their limit, because they did not improve the technologies available to farmers:

This here is the issue. It's true that the technicians of the district show us how to weed, how to sow, how to thin ... but we can't prepare the earth, this is difficult; we can only do manual work with our hands. *This is why we say that agriculture is not developing, because you need machinery to develop agriculture*, and me and my wife alone can only manage two or three hectares alone. They've already shown me how to sow, how to weed, how to sow in a line – I've learnt all this. How to keep seeds – we've learnt this. But how to plough the field? This is the difficulty, and this is why we don't go forward – because we cannot farm much land.[9]

—Farmers' forum, Nacololo

What we are missing – now we are doing manual farming, but we need help to at least have a tractor to plough the land, and then we can sow in a line, because the land would be in a condition to keep us going forward – because we have been cultivating this land for many years and the soil is tired. We are asking for them to give us a tractor so we can sow well and have a better income – not that we don't have a good income now but we can do even better ... We also don't have better seeds, or even a little manure or anything.[10]

—Farmers' forum, Netia

An agronomist responsible for training communities agreed:

Logically, when you ask why these producers have so little, even after so many years of training, I don't know. That is to say, there have been many trainings but there is no technology, *none* [emphasis in original]. So unfortunately most of our producers are still using the same technology they used in ancient Egypt. It might seem like a caricature but that is the reality.[11]

This lack of technology is compounded by the absence of any consistent agricultural extension services, which has for many years been seen as a central problem in improving productivity by a wide range of parties. One peasant representative noted that in 1984 Mozambique had around 1,200 agricultural technicians employed by the state, compared to 1,259 in 2014; a recently completed eighteen-month scheme to increase the number had not resulted in any notable increase in extensionists employed, much of the funds having been spent on workshops and seminars.[12] Another senior NGO worker commented:

> Nampula – the whole province, with 4,7 million inhabitants, the majority – 80 per cent or 90 per cent live from agriculture. And we have just 138 – one three eight – public *extensionistas* [technicians]. Badly paid, badly equipped – they probably don't even go out to the field. And like this you think that people have to open their doors to globalisation?[13]

Many of the peasant farmers interviewed had not received any public extension visits at all. Indeed, agricultural census figures reveal a significant national *fall* in numbers of farmers receiving extension visits from 13.5 per cent in 2002 to 7.7 per cent in 2008 (Cunguara and Kelly 2009: 7). Given that extension services in agriculture are central to promoting and facilitating the use of agricultural inputs, it is also then unsurprising that the numbers of farmers using improved seeds, fertilisers and pesticides is extremely low; chemical pesticide use also declined from 6.7 per cent in 2002 to 2.6 per cent in 2008 (Cunguara and Kelly 2009: 7). These inputs are, however, critical to increasing the productivity for farmers and increasing their income, which for the government and donors should be central to poverty reduction. Farmers are, however, currently in a situation where they have maximised what can be done without them. Instead, they seek ways and means of procuring such inputs themselves. One touted solution to this problem was through mechanisms for rural finance, which would provide 'market solutions' to these issues.

Rural Financing

However, a similar pattern of limited impact has been achieved with respect to microfinance – a seeming success story, in which many international NGOs and donors have been interested as a key component of poverty reduction amongst the rural poor. Whilst this vision initially aimed to increase credit to the poor in terms of loans to support expanded production, this approach initially ended up serving less poor urban clients, and with a high rate of default. Amongst the rural poor, microfinance subsequently morphed into the promotion of rotational savings and credit associations, which required no seed capital from donors but instead involved training associations in ways to generate communal savings pots from which loans could be made (de Vletter 2006). Of these, at least some have continued to function in the intended way and some members were outwardly positive about the impact on their lives. A member of a rotational savings and credit association exclaimed:

> Oh, they [the NGO] gave us a big advantage! We didn't have any vision, any idea, we were just ordinary people, walking around [gestures comically with his head down] with our heads down, not knowing anything. Then we were receiving trainers, and things became easily better. We are very thankful. We didn't know leadership. But now, thanks to God, we know how to do *associativismo* [creating associations], we have a strategic plan, an agenda.[14]

De Vletter reports that the progress of rotational savings and credit adoption has been in excess of government expectations, which had initially targeted one hundred thousand savers (2006: 2).

Yet, in terms of the effect on productivity, rotational savings and credit methods do not appear to have had a wide impact, for the most part because the funds available are insufficient to meet investment needs – that is, for extra labour or inputs (De Vletter 2006: 54). This is reflected in the national agricultural census figures recording the low use of improved inputs already discussed. Even in Nampula Province, where this initiative is considered broadly successful by many donors, the most prolific of these providers reaches just 2 per cent of the province's population on a generous count.[15]

For those reached, however, even the largest of the loans that a typical savings association might provide to a member – about US$50 – would not be enough to borrow a tractor for even one hectare of land, reported by one association at US$60.[16] There is thus a large gap between the promise of microfinance as an auto-generative source of investment and the realities of what investments can be made and by whom. Although they have promoted a more formal and more visible account of mutual help within a small number of rural communities, their capacity to transform production is limited. At best, they provide a way of reorganising the small amounts of capital that rural communities have managed to generate to better manage household needs.

A further prospective source of finance for rural communities was launched by the government in 2005 as part of a decentralisation initiative, which is commonly called the *sete milhões* (seven million) by the amount of initial investment in meticais per district (c. US$300,000). This fund was intended to stimulate local investment initiatives, based on the consultative and participatory planning mechanisms located at different levels. Whilst initially wary of the initiative, international partners became heavily involved in the provision of technical support and assistance for the project, training various people in questions of governance, planning and budgeting. The government passed further laws stipulating levels of participation and consultation that were in principle highly democratic – these were celebrated widely as evidence of a commitment to good governance and development at the local level and supported by a range of partners.

The purposes of the funds were somewhat unclear at the outset, but became understood as a larger rotational credit source for the district; the district government would provide loans to people to generate development and these loans were to be repaid (Orre et al. 2012). In the eyes of the protagonists of the policy, developed during the Guebuza administration, this was a radical departure from 'top-down' developmental models proposed by outsiders.

Yet, despite this promise of resource flow to the local level, these funds have been perceived by many of the intended beneficiaries and those interviewed for this project as inaccessible – for the most part they have been perceived as benefiting those connected to the district administrator (a post appointed by the president) or their families, or politically connected people. That they were investment funds has also been in doubt – many reported that funds were used to improve administrators' dwellings or facilities rather than for economic activity. Interviewees noted that they were not invited and excluded from decision-making regarding the funds, and others that they were not given any information about them.[17] Whilst hundreds of projects were approved, a perception is that they strengthened the hand of local government officials within the community as a source of patronage (Orre et al. 2012). In particular, some farmers reported that officials and chiefs demanded large cuts of the project money offered, thus meaning that those who sought to borrow ended up with large debts not of their making, of which they did not have the means to finance. For those telling this story, it was barely worthwhile getting all the documentation and investment plans together, which involved a huge bureaucratic struggle on their part.[18] Overall, then, efforts to provide financial aid at the level of the peasant smallholders have failed for similar reasons to efforts to increase production – they are too small, too constrained and in this case also too controlled by an unreliable state machinery.

Producing for the Market

There is a subset of interventions in rural communities, which have provided proportionately more support in terms of extension visits, inputs and technology, which have been those specifically directed at encouraging them to grow cash crops for international markets. These have been widely promoted by NGOs and social enterprises, as well as directly by the private sector. The shared vision underpinning these activities is that peasants can lift themselves out of poverty by producing more valuable crops, which will generate a monetised income stream that will stimulate rural development.

Typically, starter packages provided by these interventions will include a supply of certified seeds in the relevant crop, training in how to sow and plant, plus support for creation of an association to facilitate sales and storage. These programmes, usually three years in length, will include multiple visits during the project cycle plus monitoring and evaluation activity. More ambitious programmes in Nampula have involved creating a co-operative social enterprise to buy from farmers' associations and sell to the international market, cutting out private middlemen (*intervenientes*). These interventions are explicitly directed at improving the supply chain as a means of raising farmer incomes.

However, understood from the point of view of the beneficiaries, these interventions have still left them in highly precarious situations, mostly because there are no consistent or predictable purchasing arrangements for the crops, despite the promises of higher incomes by the NGOs, social enterprises and companies promoting it. Every farmer group interviewed raised this issue – that they tried to follow the schemes but were mostly let down when it came to sell:

This year, we tried to do cotton – we were being told by everyone that this is 'white gold', so we were all making, planting, harvesting … but for this 'white gold', we were getting 6 MT [$0.28 USD] per kilo! We couldn't buy anything.[19]
—Farmers' savings and credit association, Monapo

It didn't get better, because roaming vendors bring their own scales and just say the price at which they want to buy. 'I'm going to buy this at this price'. So, as a peasant with my own concerns I am forced to sell, because I have difficulties, because I have to send my child to school. This is an issue, the lack of the market, because if you had a market this wouldn't happen.[20]
—Peasant farmer provincial representatives

If you show up there with an association, you have to look at the environment of the community. If it's a peasant association, you have to understand why it was formed. I can't just show up there and create an association because I'm bringing seeds tomorrow. This is what has created some distortions. If you say 'Antonio, what are you planting? Tomatoes? Why don't you also plant some soya?' Because this soya is like this, and does this, and they try to understand beforehand. And they understand that one day they will ask, 'Is it true that if I produce, there will be buyers? Who will buy it? Are you sure of this? And this year, if not, what will I do with this soya?' These are discussions which we have not had carefully.[21]
—Peasant farmer provincial representatives

Hasn't anyone tried to bring these things [tractors, improved seeds] here?
No! There's a cotton company called SAN but they only give you cotton seeds … and they said they would not plough any fields unless we planted only cotton.
Would you like to plant cotton?
No! We stopped because it gave us a lot of hassle … you have to weed it six times and it doesn't give much profit – it just brings hunger.[22]
—Farmers' forum, Netia

This difficulty takes place so much at the level of producers with middlemen and buyers – there is no signing of a contract. Because before, they used to say they would buy and they had to bring a contract with the producers in the period of production. He can then plan, knowing that I'm going to do X hectares of crop X, because I'm going to sell to that guy, but this isn't happening.[23]

—Farmers' forum, Nacololo

Many of the groups interviewed had been encouraged to cultivate sesame by a well-regarded social enterprise co-founded by international organisations, and many had reported successes in the early years of production. As noted by the interveners' documentation, per kilo, sesame attracts a relatively high price on the international market (US$2.50/kg), and the established enterprise successfully purchased and resold the crop in the mid-2000s. It can be intercropped with food, meaning the risk of food shortage is less than with monocultures such as cotton. International agencies invested heavily in projects to engage and improve the 'supply value chain' for this crop and have spent millions of dollars training for this.

Yet, farmer experiences of production suggest that the promise of improving their conditions through such a crop may be short-lived. Sesame is a crop which is highly labour-intensive in terms of harvesting, predictably introduces disease within a year or two without the use of pesticides, loses moisture and mass if not sold on time, and is vulnerable to storage infestation when not stored securely. One agronomist interviewed said that it could be grown only for four years from the starting conditions, and then one had to do something else.[24] For various reasons, the interventions established were not geared up or able to deal with these issues, leaving many of those interviewed frustrated. Some had stopped producing it, some had stopped selling it to the social enterprise due to conflicts over timing and predictability, and others continued to produce and to sell in reduced quantities but with ongoing concerns both on this front and regarding the market. One farmer noted a drop from 800 kg per hectare to 300 kg due to lack of irrigation and production means, and others complained that facilities that had been promised, such as for storage, had never been delivered.

Overall, the picture from the experience of producing for the market at the encouragement of intervention is thus deeply mixed, with interventions often acting somewhat irresponsibly. For peasant farmers, when prices are good, the harvest is good and the crop sells on time and predictably, there is clearly satisfaction and happiness derived from that. However, it is also clear that there are a wide range of potential and predictable pitfalls which interveners have either been unwilling or unable to address, and peasants have borne the costs of having either unsold or unsellable crops, diseased or infested crops, monopolistic and unfair purchase arrangements, lack of transport, storage and the other stresses of uncertainty.

***

Whilst Mozambique did appear to be a major success story for developmental intervention on the part of donors in the first years following the end of the war, since then rural development has slowed down seriously and is on some indicators going 'backwards' in terms of productivity. Recent studies suggest that absolute poverty has in fact *increased* (Cunguara et al. 2012) despite its macroeconomic growth, and this is due to the collapse in rural productivity per head. From the perspectives of peasant farmers – without formal education in agronomy or development economics, or overviews of agricultural statistics and censuses – this is obvious given the lack of investment in agricultural services, supplies and technology, and lack of stable markets. It is also obvious to some of those delivering the interventions as subcontractors to the donors:

> The type of help given by most of the donors – I think it doesn't work ... To continue using a flip chart and marker all the time, that is to say that the producers have been seeing this for ten, fifteen years. They see a new technician coming on a motorbike but it's the same old thing. So imagine – I am feeling this and the producers are also feeling the same thing. The same technologies. Since the war ended in Mozambique in 1992, 1993, the teaching techniques are the same. So our producers who are fifty years old – they who are seeing, they who have been hearing the same thing for twenty years, the same story until now when they are 50. So something is not going well with how we are doing things. This is not right.[25]
> —Agricultural enterprise manager

> There are organisations that only came and formed associations. For me the concern was that they formed a thousand and such associations, legalised them and then said we have already done the work. You leave, the names remain, but these associations you are looking for cannot be found. So that's the point, at least me, that's how I see it ... That money, if you evaluate the investment, is millions of dollars. But when we are going to evaluate who was left, at least one person doing such an activity does not exist.[26]
> —Peasant farmer provincial representatives

On the ground, the limitations of policy and interventions in the agricultural sector indeed seem obvious. The question then becomes, what has been going on politically over the last twenty years, such that this is what has resulted? And where has the money gone? The following section outlines the development of agricultural policy in the post-war period, as negotiated between the Government of Mozambique and its assorted partners. As with health, there has been a significant and systematic fragmentation of efforts and resources, which have followed around areas of fashionable interest and political significance – international, regional and national – rather than the cumulative development of mass provision in areas of ongoing basic need. This has resulted in erratic provision, sudden changes in policy direction and a deterioration of co-ordination mechanisms.

AGRICULTURAL POLICIES, THE STATE AND INTERNATIONAL INTERVENTION

> I feel that donors don't really want to reduce poverty. We started with PROAGRI in 1995 [*sic*]. There were millions spent on consultant studies – four studies, but if you see how much is going to the farmer, it's just 25% – I say why? Each donor wants to do the study, and to use the money of PROAGRI. And the amount of money they pay for the study is unacceptable. They always want the evaluation, and they contract out – and how much do they support? But the support for the farmers itself, they are not getting a lot. With one study, you can buy ten tractors, you can really solve some problems.[27]
>
> —Former agricultural technician working for
> European donor agency

The structural adjustment plan that Mozambique signed up to in 1987, in order to qualify for Western financial assistance, affected the agricultural sector as it did many others. The budget for salaries to public sector technicians was dramatically cut, and took a while to recover (Mosca 2011: 109). Prices were liberalised, the currency was devalued, meaning more competitive exports but more expensive imports, credit to state-owned enterprises was drastically lowered and many large agricultural enterprises were privatised through sales to politically connected figures and international investors. Agricultural production increased as a result of population return after the war and the broader expectation on the part of the donors was that market activity would stimulate and drive economic development. As already noted, many NGOs entered the country with the stated objectives of helping peasants link better to the markets.

In terms of international statebuilding efforts, the push by donors to reform and build the capacity of the Ministry of Agriculture and Rural Development (MADER) became a major focus of activity. A common fund (PROAGRI) was established in 1999, under the principles of direct budget support, to help consolidate funding for the ministry. The stated emphasis within this first phase (1999–2005) was capacity-building, improving production and supporting natural resources. Of this, as is widely understood, the vast majority of funds was spent on institution-building within the ministry and (often outsourced) research, with relatively little going to the provision of services to farmers (Evans et al. 2007: 26). Moreover, a high proportion of these funds was also spent at the central level instead of at the provincial or district level. What is less widely reported is that the majority of the state officials who were supposed to be trained under PROAGRI did not complete the training (Government of Mozambique 2007: ix), and, as with the health sector, a large number left to work for donors and NGOs on their own agricultural strategies and programmes. The result is a state apparatus for agriculture that is fragmented and poorly staffed despite the investment of millions of dollars, particularly at the provincial and district levels but also at the centre.

A further emphasis of donors and government – driven more on a project basis – was in encouraging the growth of large-scale agribusinesses, although these have not produced any transformation in the conditions for the majority of peasants. Many of these sought to revive colonial-era enterprises and plantations, such as in coconuts, sugar and sisal. Others sought to establish large areas for new crops, such as jatropha, eucalyptus and soya, through either a plantation or an outgrower model. Many of these were supported by the government unit Centre for the Promotion of Agriculture (CEPAGRI), which housed a number of international economists as well as government officials and was engaged in promoting strategic crops. There are research institutes for cotton, sugar and cashew, which were also connected to these efforts. However, whilst these units and forms of co-operation conducted much research and established many strategies, the impact on the ground was highly variable.

On the one hand, they managed to attract a series of prospective investors, and some enterprises were rehabilitated successfully. For example, the colonial-era Sena Sugar Estates at Marromeu was taken over by a consortium of Mauritian and South African investors, but, crucially, the investment was underwritten by the World Bank. In total, the sugar industry has seen US$300 million invested in the last twenty years and has succeeded in exporting to the EU, which has been tariff-free for African, Caribbean and Pacific (ACP) producers, although the future is unclear given the recent change in the tariff regime. On the other hand, a more disastrous intervention took place in coconut plantations, where in Zambezia the US Government–funded Millennium Challenge Account and its private and NGO subcontractors ignored warnings of producers and local experts about disease and pests and pressed on with the project they had designed. These then destroyed the entire plantation and affected the nearby family sector (Valoi 2013). The government's rapid promotion of jatropha as a crop for biodiesel export also is seen to have failed, with peasants complaining that no one had bought it despite tons being produced at the behest of the then president (Macauhub 2010). Over the longer term, little attention has been paid to the creation of rural jobs, despite this being highlighted early on as significant (Cramer and Pontara 1998).

By the end of the first PROAGRI programme in 2005, the government was under pressure from rising food prices and disappointments about production and support to the family sector. Moreover, many investments in agribusiness which had had international support through the CEPAGRI unit of government did not pan out successfully or produce sufficient jobs. One of the early decisions of the Guebuza administration in 2005 was to convert MADER into the Ministry of Agriculture (MINAG) and put rural development in the Ministry of Planning and Development. The second PROAGRI programme (2007–12) emphasised good governance, transparency and decentralisation, and it also received initial support from many of the donors who had supported the first programme. With the declaration that the district level was to be the 'pole of development', the *sete milhões* (seven million meticais) local investment initiative proceeded as an exemplar of many international priorities in planning and participation.

At a political level, there was understood to be a 'change of paradigm' on agricultural policy (Eurosis 2010: 86) within the government in favour of 'food security'. This was ostensibly aimed at being more 'pro-poor' and 'pro-peasant'. The administration aligned itself with initiatives such as the Green Revolution for Africa (2007) and the African Union Comprehensive Africa Agriculture Development Programme (CAADP) initiative. These committed it to an expansion of public funding for agriculture, an investment in technologies for production as well as infrastructures. In planning terms, a Food Production Action Plan (PAPA) was launched in 2007 for 2008–11, followed by a Strategic Plan for Agricultural Development (PEDSA) to last from 2010 to 2019. This was accompanied by a CAADP Strategy known as the National Plan for Strategic Investment in Agriculture 2014–18 (PNISA).

However, many donors, including the World Bank and USAID, pulled out of direct support for the agricultural sector with this change of direction, unhappy with the prospect of direct subsidy for or provision of inputs to the farming sector, as well as the proliferation of different strategies (Government of Mozambique 2010: 56–57). The donors redoubled efforts within the private sector following this fallout, emphasising agribusiness, supply chain linkages and cash crops as primary paths to agricultural development. The amount of assistance channelled through PROAGRI has fallen dramatically – from a peak of 64 per cent in 2005 to 32 per cent in 2009 (Government of Mozambique 2010: 58), directly as a result of the struggle over these policies and priorities. The dynamics of *protagonismo* identified in the previous chapter then emerged strongly with regard to the agricultural sector, with each donor seeking to make its own impact and headway in an area of its choosing.

The Government of Mozambique's own published assessment is that international co-operation in agriculture was, in comparative terms, *less successful* than that in the health sector. It can be seen that there are similar dynamics in terms of the effect of intervention on the state sector to those described in the previous chapter – the fragmentation of resource and capacities, the lack of delivery on the ground, the focus on specific activities with political importance (e.g. HIV/AIDS and some cash crops) and tensions between the donors and government over priorities. Evidence that policies were not having a transformative impact has been abundantly supplied through agricultural surveys, crop-specific research and an array of reports and evaluations. Moreover, the basic lack of resources to accomplish even a small proportion of the stated objectives has been a chronic issue which has not yet shown improvement. It is for these reasons that leading Mozambican agronomist João Mosca has recently argued that 'there has never been an agricultural policy' in Mozambique (Caldeira 2016). He argues in a long-term analysis of agricultural policy that chronic and severe underinvestment, political fragmentation and instability, the lack of institutional capacity and technical knowledge have systematically undermined efforts to develop the sector (Mosca 2011: chapter 7).

Yet, perhaps more fundamentally, there has been within the agricultural sector – more so with some donors than the government – a specific ideological firewall against sustained and direct state support for the family sector and the kinds of support that peasants have said that they need, even to fulfil the objectives of market participation and integration. In limited situations, some private companies have established contracts and support agreements that act to mitigate risk for small farmers, such as in tobacco (Hanlon et al. 2008). Yet, the donors are fundamentally reluctant, even when the evidence is there, to allow for the state to mitigate risks to the family sector. In a recent analysis of the government's CAADP investment strategy, Thurlow (2013) argues that input subsidies and better extension services have a much better potential for increasing productivity than the suggested focus on irrigation. Although the government's recent 'paradigm change' signals that they are willing to move in this direction of better subsidising and resourcing peasant production, it is unclear that they can do so in practice without a corresponding transformative change in the institutional environment or political dialogue. According to Mozambican academic observers, the proliferation of initiatives and strategies is embedded primarily in a quest to maximise the inflow of resources (Mosca 2011; Castel-Branco 2007) rather than being an articulation of a sustained policy direction.

To put these developments into the light of the findings of the previous section, whilst the peasants have been the object of specific but rather limited programmes over the last twenty years, the machinery of public policy has become fragmented, contested and overlaid with a range of political conflicts and projects from both donors and government. Underpinned by the relations of asymmetry and dependency described in the previous chapter, the government has nonetheless been less willing to concede political ground in this sector to the donors, leaving relations and resource flows heavily stilted. Donors, for their part, have been unwilling to confront the often hypocritical and counter-productive character of their own policy prescriptions, refusing forms of support which are widely used elsewhere. Despite the mounting evidence that there are serious and urgent problems at the level of agricultural production, demonstrated through the national surveys, the political deadlock on the issue combined with the fragmentation of the state means that it is unlikely to be resolved soon. Much will depend, then, on whether other partners, such as producer states from the global South, will provide the space and resources to work around this.

That said, international assistance flowed not only to the state sector within agriculture but also to civil society organisations representing the rights and interests of peasants. These organisations have had a significant impact on key developments in the agricultural sector over the last twenty years, particularly with regard to land tenure. These are being seen as increasingly prescient given present pressures on land from both elite domestic investors and their foreign counterparts (UNAC/GRAIN 2015). In the next section, I contemplate the significance of these forms of co-operation as part of the intervention landscape and note that these represent alternative departures for thinking about assistance. In particular, they offer an alternative vision of how to organise production such that it serves the needs of peasant farmers first.

THE PEASANT MOVEMENT AND ALTERNATIVE VISIONS OF DEVELOPMENT

Whilst the political struggles between the government and donors on agricultural policy has been played out over the last two or three decades, a mobilised, well-connected and materially funded network of organisations representing peasants and their interests has created some political force in terms of rethinking the political landscape. Their presence is a constant thorn in the side of both the government and donors, and increasingly they are at the forefront of resistance to the seemingly more progressive forms of co-operation between Southern governments (e.g. Brazil) and Mozambique. Whilst these movements began life as a campaign around questions of land tenure and reform, they have become institutionalised as a counterpoint to the extraverted strategies of rural development pursued by both donors and the government. I look here at the questions of land tenure and food sovereignty, which are key planks of its alternative thinking on rural production and development.[28]

In the early 1990s, the National Union of Peasant Farmers (UNAC) and the Organisation for Rural Mutual Assistance (ORAM) were formed and, from their inception, had a particular interest in the question of land reform. They were materially supported by a number of the Scandinavian donors and have since received work from USAID and DfID, amongst others. They are also linked to global movements such as the *Via Campesina* and *Movimento Sem Terra* (MST) in Brazil. They have often been supported by academic organisations and think tanks – such as the Institute for Social and Economic Studies (IESE), Academic Action for the Development of Rural Communities (ADECRU) and *Cruzeiro do Sul* – that produce regular analyses of government and donor policy. These organisations are also partially funded by international agencies – mostly small European donors. Although not widely visible and read by the broader population for numerous reasons, their analyses and engagements frequently make it into the national press; they provide a source of high-quality intellectual labour for the policy world, and their members rotate through public universities and international conferences. Whilst they do not officially promote any specific political platform, they have, often in collaboration with the peasant organisations, challenged government and donor thinking on questions of poverty reduction, agricultural productivity, land grabs and foreign investment, privatisation, aid and state ownership and social protection.

On the question of land, in the post-war period it was widely known and expected that this central plank of public policy – the allocation of land to and by the state – would be under pressure from the donors who would want privatisation for the purposes of foreign investment. However, a large campaign ensued, led by UNAC, ORAM and other organisations, resulting in the Land Law of 1997, which established community and/or individual rights to land they had been farming for ten years and specified a process of consultation on any resettlement proposals and compensation for people displaced. Individuals and communities can register a Direito do Uso e Aproveitamento da Tarra (DUAT) (a right of usage for land) but the law underwrites their claim, even if they have not done so.

In relative terms, this is the most pro-poor land law in Africa. Whilst this has not stopped all processes of displacement which do not comply, in principle there has been the capacity to do so, which seems to have been factored into agribusiness planning. On some limited occasions, peasants have also successfully challenged enterprises who have not complied. For example, in Nampula Province, Lurio Green Resources was challenged by the community in conjunction with the local government after having conducted a very shallow consultation and forced to redo the process.[29] At a national level, widespread concerns emerged about the proposals for PROSAVANA – a huge project with Brazilian and Japanese investors designed to cultivate soya in the Nacala corridor. Significant demonstrations and forms of resistance took place at both national and community levels, meaning the project has been effectively stalled for the foreseeable future. Whilst the government at a

central level is very clearly frustrated, and the public remains uncertain as to
what is coming next, it is clear that vocal and organised civil resistance has
slowed down projects like this. It has done so by capitalising on the symbolic
and political importance of the peasantry to the wider political establishment
in the country, and in particular that central connection to the land which was
the promise of the liberation struggle.

The peasant movements have also been active in promoting a campaign
around 'food sovereignty', which is aimed at challenging the government's
vision for the involvement of corporate suppliers and large-scale plantations
in the delivery of 'food security'. This 'food sovereignty' campaign endorsed
by UNAC in Mozambique articulates more clearly the connections between
the central endorsement of particular production strategies in agriculture and
the exclusion of the peasantry from their formulation. In particular, UNAC
and other coalition partners have attacked plans such as the Green Revolution
for Africa, publicly endorsed by the president as a means of ensuring 'food
security', for their failure to engage with the existing modes of production
and needs of peasant farmers. They argue that these would be better served
by a more supportive market for locally produced goods rather than imports,
and more attention to land access (Nhampossa 2007).

Within this 'food sovereignty' campaign is an alternative vision of how
Mozambique should engage with the world and how the state should engage with
the peasantry. In short, it calls for a substantial reorientation of Mozambique's
development strategies around consumer and producer meetings, community
co-ordination and non-intensive agriculture as ways of connecting peasant
autonomy with economic survival.[30] As UNAC argue, rising food prices in
particular have contributed to not just rural poverty but also broader patterns of
alienation in Mozambique's cities. In particular, a reliance on wheat imports has
rendered urban populations susceptible to world food price and currency fluctua-
tions, contributing, along with fuel prices, to increased social unrest and rioting
in recent years (BBC News 2010). It is perhaps not a little ironic that some of
the money that funds development interventions in Mozambique derives directly
from the sale of US wheat surpluses into this market.[31]

Although the food sovereignty terminology has not become politically
mainstream in Mozambique, the campaign and pressure on questions of food
production arguably has created a context in which the post-2010 government policy for food production has had to respond to its criticisms. The
food sovereignty discourse rearticulates the problems of the contemporary
economic system through lenses which speak to the historic situation of the
peasantry. As articulated by the farmers interviewed for this project, and also
noted in the Chr. Michelsen Institute's (CMI) studies of rural poverty, these
strategies very rarely depend on the state or NGOs for income or social insurance (Tvedten et al. 2006). Although the food sovereignty movement does

not rule out a role for state intervention, the vision speaks to the need more fundamentally to reconfigure the relations between people, the state and the market. This speaks to an ambivalent relationship with state-led development strategies in the territory and the tendency for these to be oriented towards extraverted development models. As we will see in the next section, these have had only limited advantages for the peasantry.

Taken together, the presence and activity of the peasant movements and their supporters are significant for three reasons in thinking about the debates on international intervention. First, it is a demonstration that public account-ability can function even with donors in the picture and that they still have the ability to force climbdowns or changes of direction on specific issues. To this extent, 'democracy' needs to be understood outside the formal framework of parliamentary opposition and more as a set of struggles for the public nar-rative. Second, it is clear that international assistance can, *when it chooses*, support efforts that seem to have genuinely 'pro-poor' or 'pro-peasant' conse-quences, and ones which are critical of its own presence. Although this is not the norm and it is largely the Nordic countries that do this for historic reasons, it becomes clearer that options exist for such kinds of engagement. Third, it is also clear that emerging from the work that organisations such as UNAC and IESE do is a different vision of what 'development' and well-being can mean, especially when understood from the point of view of peasant farmers. In this other vision, development and well-being begins from and is grounded in the creation of conditions for mutual support and uplift, the valuing of people at the base and the orientation of systems in line with their needs.

This different vision resonates further when located in an appreciation of the historical dynamics of political organisation and production within rural Mozambique, which has been shaped by globalising forces for centuries. In this longer historical perspective, the need for these alternative understand-ings of democracy and development rooted in an engagement with the base becomes particularly pressing in light of the ways in which the peasantry has been chronically marginalised from political and economic projects. Worse, it has been subjected to forms of destabilisation and experimentation over time which have destroyed and left fragile the social and economic fabric of rural communities. It is these to which we now turn to locate our understanding of intervention and its effect on the peasantry.

THE MOZAMBICAN PEASANTRY AND
THE LONG VIEW OF INTERVENTION

The post-war interventions in Mozambique have tended to start from a base which understands their arrival as effectively a Year Zero in terms of development. Duffield describes this orientation as interveners projecting a sense of 'the cleansing fire of war' having stripped African populations back to being part of a bare, natural economy which is essentially self-sustaining and self-reproducing (2007: 90). As argued in chapter 1, many critical scholars in the global North also leave this assumption undisturbed through their failure to historicise populations subject to international statebuilding. What happens when such histories are brought into view? One important understanding that emerges is that the peasantry in Mozambique are not recent but long-term subjects of global political and economic forces that have by turns integrated, dispossessed and then ignored them. It is not a lack of connectedness that characterises this dynamic so much as the basic structural indifference of external parties to their conditions which is the continuous feature. To this extent, the experiences of post-war intervention amongst the peasantry have not showed a transformation in conditions, even if interveners' ideals and promises formally reject the policies of the not-so-distant past and present themselves as 'pro-poor'.

Northern Mozambique carries both physical and political imprints of its long historical integration with the rest of the world. Ruined buildings, trading posts, churches and factories can be found along the coast of Nampula Province, for example, as can the large fortress on Mozambique Island which served as the route for the export of enslaved Africans until the late nineteenth century. Further inland, although fewer in number and density, ruins of colonial-era farm buildings, estates and equipment are also present. Other zones in the north were under the control – sometimes more nominal than profound – of colonial companies, who operated under royal charters and with full right to 'develop' the country's potential for export markets. This also entailed a claimed sovereign right to raise hut taxes and/or take forced labour (*chibalo*) as a way of payment from African populations.

As Portuguese colonialism intensified, expanded territorially and reorganised itself in the twentieth century, an administrative system developed in which district-level organisation and *régulos* ('traditional' leaders) were created. Combined with *sipais* (native policemen), this administrative structure expanded the capacity of a now unitary state to collect taxes, enforce the cultivation of crops such as cotton, and take people seen as 'immoral' or 'idle' to work on large infrastructure projects, sometimes very far from their homes. Others were encouraged to migrate to provide seasonal labour in the South African mines or to take industrial work in the south of the country. In all of these processes, the African peasantry in Mozambique were seen as a resource to exploit or 'develop', either as human assets to be commodified and traded or as productive assets which could be targeted for labour, specific crops and products.

Significantly, the networks and needs which they served were *global* in terms of commodity chains and transnational in terms of being woven into several imperial systems of production. Labour was also moved globally – through the trade in bonded humans to the Americas and in the rotation of migrant labour to South Africa. In this sense, the Mozambican peasantry has been intensively connected to the system of the modern global market for at least a hundred years, and long before the presence of the liberal post-war development and statebuilding projects.

Yet, this integration into global processes was also mediated through significant forms of counter-organisation and resistance, which also enjoyed transnational connections and support. Isaacman and Isaacman (1976) elaborate an array of forms of anti-colonial resistance from the nineteenth century onwards to the 1920s in the centre of the country, which included forms of evasion, migration, the establishment of alliances and open-armed rebellion. There was also significant resistance to the forced cotton regime from the 1930s onwards (Isaacman et al. 1980; Isaacman 1995) which also involved forms of crop sabotage amongst other strategies. More obviously, the anti-colonial liberation front (Frelimo) which emerged in the 1960s in Tanzania spread through the north of Mozambique and advocated openly for the overthrow of the Portuguese regime, in collaboration with a wider global anti-colonial movement. As did other guerrilla movements, Frelimo faced violent repression and sought shelter amongst the population, leading to attacks by the colonial powers on the same.

As far as peasant life was concerned, independence brought both changes and continuities. Frelimo's anti-colonial purge dislodged many of the traditional authorities (*régulos*) installed by the Portuguese and put in place local party infrastructures and *Grupos Dinamizadores* to organise social and political life. The experience of this varied widely across the country; whilst many were supportive and enthusiastic, much of the ideological orthodoxy was either illegible or irrelevant to the people and realities of the situation (Marshall 1993; Harrison 2000). It also had a number of coercive elements in different parts of the country. Particularly when Renamo appeared (Cahen 1987), populations were contained in collective villages to prevent infiltration, but these were also schemes to resettle rural populations in order to make them 'develop' and produce in different ways (Coelho 1998).[32] However, given the fragility of the postcolonial state and its dependence on foreign exchange, to some extent similar policies were produced – Samora Machel called on peasants to produce cotton as a national duty, for example, despite its continued unpopularity.[33] The attempts to expand assistance to the peasants also faced severe capacity constraints, which meant that, as now, the survival and reproduction of rural populations was ensured for the large part by their own efforts.

What is interesting about the transitions from colonialism to independence, and from socialism to liberalism, is that both incorporated widespread *de-development* and de-industrialisation, as a result of active sabotage and human capital flight as well as weaknesses in public decision-making.[34] When the majority of Portuguese settlers left in 1975, for example, it was in a hurry and people were not permitted to evacuate with many belongings. There are many examples of industries and enterprises having their records burnt, estates and equipment destroyed and sabotaged, more or less simply out of spite. The same goes for a number of homes. Enterprises such as sugar and copra manufacturing which were established and functional virtually ceased to function, as did much of the technological infrastructure in the agricultural sector, such as there was. The colonial power saw itself as having invested in the lands it possessed, and there was no desire amongst many of the settlers to see it flourish after they had left.[35]

The war with Renamo was, similarly, both *anti-public sector* and *anti-developmental* in strategy and effects, designed to precipitate the failure of the government. In this sense, it provides a counter-narrative to the idea that 'wars make states' – in Mozambique for the peasants, this was not the case. In particular the extensive landmining of the rural areas and the sabotage of enterprises, roads and railways actively targeted the capacities of the state to support and rule the peasantry, as well as the peasantry to be able to put their own coping mechanisms such as migration and counter-mobilisations into effect. This strategy of sabotage was necessary, for Renamo's white minority backers in Rhodesia and South Africa, to demonstrate that a black African socialist frontline state should not be able to succeed unchallenged. It was also incidental insofar as Renamo's own capacities were not particularly well organised or co-ordinated – they were not particularly interested in building their own 'liberated zones' with ideas for social and political organisation or production. Instead, they reinstated a number of the colonial chiefs and demanded supplies but did little else in terms of stimulating production. It is significant that in this Cold War 'proxy war', the main objective was to *produce political and economic failure* through a campaign of violence.

The end of the war in 1990, peace, liberalisation, concerted efforts at statebuilding and the international NGO explosion, however, promised an improvement in this situation for the peasants. After all, here were the world's wealthiest countries, most experienced technical consultants and most prestigious institutions to offer development resources, expertise and more amenable conditions in which to improve the lives of the peasantry. Surely, in the absence of war and colonialism – two phenomena directly counterposed to the peace and freedom offered by liberal intervention – such efforts should have been richly rewarded? As testified by farmers and studies, however, productivity is lower than in colonial times despite twenty years of such efforts.

How can we make sense of this? On the one hand, there is the fragmenting effect that international intervention has had on the state infrastructure and strategies of production. As with the health sector in the post-war period, there are multiple dynamics and processes which actively push resources, capacity and energy *away* from public investment in agriculture, precluding any accumulation thereof. This is not the same as the colonial and socialist orders, which at least sought to instrumentally accumulate capacity in these areas. West's (2008) account of the post-1990 reforms as an experience of political and economic 'abandonment' amongst the peasantry resonates strongly with this characterisation.

Another factor is the extremely short-termist nature of the interventions themselves and their desires for quick and visible results. In this sense, sesame can be understood as the international NGO crop *par excellence* given its quick yields but predictable long-term degradation of the crop and soil. Higher forms of investment and inputs would be needed to maintain 'success', but they are not forthcoming from any particular source. Moreover, for projects or programmes to succeed in the sector, investments of at least ten years would be desirable.[36] A further factor has been the active suppression by international interveners of efforts to subsidise inputs and create price stabilisation for farmers or state marketing arrangements that might have mitigated risk for the rural poor (Smart et al. 2014) – which even colonial and socialist production methods managed to different degrees. This is in spite of the fact that such donors do the opposite for their own markets – as noted, much US Government funding to the agricultural sector in Mozambique occurs through the Title II Food for Peace mechanism – that is, the sale of agricultural surpluses into the local market bought by the US Government from US producers.

Whilst not a strategy of destruction *per se*, international intervention over the last twenty to thirty years has shown a *determined and structural indifference* to its own repeated failures, a ready propensity to consume its own resources as well as active antipathy towards policies that might give the state a central supportive role in the agricultural sector. Whilst much energy and money has been put towards the generation of studies, evaluations, strategies, capacities and plans by interveners, which in many instances require farmer participation to fulfil, there is very little to show at the level of the population beyond unsteady returns, disappointed expectations, limited amounts of temporary resource and ongoing exposure to malnutrition.

And yet, the potential paths to development are clearly visible to the peasantry and have been so for some time. They can see across the landscape of the country industrial farmers with more and better machinery, individuals, groups and organisations with appropriate levels of financing for investment, individuals with the right kinds of education and so on. The things which would be necessary to uplift their situation clearly exist and are available for the right price, making it all the more frustrating that the projects which come to 'develop' them never exactly deliver this. What is lacking is not the means of production *per se*, but the capacity to appropriate it for themselves.

It is in this context that the peasant movement emphasis described in the previous section on reorienting development comes into view. By articulating a vision of uplift rooted in those resources – particularly land – over which peasants have relative control, and a vision for their critical resource – that is, food – the alternative priorities for development seek to insure against the structures of external indifference to which the peasantry has been historically subject. Rather, by recentring peasant production and control as the main elements of a development strategy, they hope to reconnect the missions of liberation and development to their intended subjects. To decolonise the gaze here is to rethink how intervention, solidarity and assistance would work in a world which put such issues at the forefront of its aims.

***

For the rural populations, twenty years of international assistance have had some successes, as discussed in the last chapter, particularly in terms of extending the reach of basic public services such as schools and hospitals. In terms of supporting a broad-based agricultural development strategy which transforms the poor conditions of the peasantry, however, there has been little movement. This is not to say that 'development' has only been 'virtual' or 'ineffective', although the mismatch between its projections in reports and its reality is profound. Rather, we must contemplate the idea that interventional intervention itself has operated in a way in which its reported successes follow directly from and are dependent on the suppression and ignoring of these realities. It is through a re-engagement of the historical presence, political consciousness and material realities of the peasants that such an interpretation becomes available. In this framework, the peasants are both symbolically necessary and materially disposable to the perceived successes of intervention. Yet, it is also possible to emphasise modes of engagement that would begin from the realities and historical situation of the peasants themselves.

In the previous two chapters, using our decolonising strategies, we have seen that, viewed from the ground, intervention can be understood as fragmenting and disorderly, hypocritical and indifferent to its ultimate effects on its intended beneficiaries, whom it treats as disposable. These perspectives are made available by an engagement with the targets of intervention, a sense of their historical presence, their political consciousness and their material realities. These deny the intellectual tendency to see interveners themselves and their activities as the key terrain of the political but insist upon reading them within a landscape populated by other people, projects and ideas. It is only then that questions of the *costs* of intervention can begin to be calculated in terms of its wider impact on the lives of targets.

In the next chapter, we open up further alternative interpretations of intervention through an engagement with the politics of anti-corruption. By engaging our decolonising strategies, the politics of intervention is woven into public discourses on greed and corruption as part of an inter-dependent moral economy, which challenges the claims of intervention to be promoting 'good governance'. Within this wider ethical landscape, intervention cannot escape its own situatedness within structures of accu-mulation and dispossession, obligation and entitlement, and labour and reward, which problematise the visions of statebuilding and development to which it is attached.

NOTES

1. Interview with farmers' group, Anchilo district, Nampula, 29 July 2014.

2. This means they own less than ten hectares of land, ten cattle, fifty goats, pigs or sheep, and 5,000 chickens (Ministry of Agriculture 2007).

3. See Stiglitz (1998).

4. This can be seen in the 2009 Frelimo manifesto, amongst other places. Retrieved on 5 September 2011 from http://www.frelimo-online.org.

5. Interview with peasant farmers' union representatives, Nampula, 5 August 2014.

6. Interview with farmers' association, Nampula, Monapo district, 7 August 2014.

7. Interview with social enterprise employee, Nampula, Anchilo district, 30 July 2014.

8. Ibid.

9. Interview with farmers' forum, Nampula, Monapo district, 6 August 2014.

10. Interview with farmers' forum, Nampula, 7 August 2014.

11. Interview with senior agricultural technician-turned-manager, Nampula, 25 July 2014.

12. Interview with peasant farmer representative, Nampula, 2 August 2014.

13. Interview with senior agricultural technician-turned-manager, Nampula, 25 July 2014.

14. Interview with savings and credit association, Nampula, Monapo district, 7 August 2009.

15. Interview with savings and credit training provider, Nampula, 31 July 2014.

16. Interview with farmers' forum, Nampula, Monapo district, 6 August 2014.

17. Orre et al. (2012); various interviews.

18. Interview with farmers' forum, Nampula, 7 August 2014.

19. Interview with farmers' savings and credit association, Nampula, Monapo district, 7 August 2009.

20. Interview with peasant farmers' union representatives, Nampula, 5 August 2014.

21. Ibid.

22. Interview with farmers' forum, Nampula, 7 August 2014.

23. Interview with farmers' forum, Nampula, 7 August 2014.

24. Interview with agricultural technician employed by European co-operation agency, 7 July 2009.

25. Interview with senior agricultural technician-turned-manager, Nampula, 25 July 2014.

26. Interview with peasant farmers' union representatives, Nampula, 5 August 2014.

27. Interview with senior agricultural technician, Beira, 7 July 2009.

28. See also Dunford (2015).

29. Interview with civil society representative, Nampula, 31 July 2014.

30. UNAC representative Ismael Ossemane, Reported in FoodFirst Magazine (2009), Conference on the Green Revolution in Mozambique. Retrieved 25 August 2011 from http://www.foodfirst.org/en/node/1781.

31. For a longer assessment of the impact, see Donovan et al. (2010).

32. This villagisation programme clearly resonates with the Tanzanian experiment in *ujaamaa* and Soviet-era gigantism. See Scott (1998), chapters 6 and 7.

33. Rahul Rao reminds me that this is not dissimilar to the situation of Toussaint L'Ouverture regarding the production of sugar in Haiti after the expulsion of the French.

34. See also Turner et al. (2014) on 'de-development'.

35. Some settlers, particularly young and politically engaged settlers, chose to stay and gave virtually all of their wealth and possessions over to 'the Revolution'. Interview with former public sector health worker, 22 June 2009.

36. Interview with senior agricultural economist, Maputo, 12 August 2014.

Chapter Six

Anti-Corruption and the Limits of Intervention

> Another thing is that local workers and international workers for an organisation have a big difference in contractual conditions. They treat people as nationals and internationals – and what is the justification? They say we base the pay on what is in Europe ... When basic needs are met, it's ok ... of course I am going to do my job, *but if I ask, between me and you, what's the difference?*
>
> —Former agricultural technician working for
> European donor agency[1]

What was the difference between my interviewee and his European colleague? Although they were doing similar jobs, she was much younger, less experienced, and, she admitted separately, earning much more money and living much better than she could have done in her own country. I was not exactly surprised by the question but found it disturbing for a long time afterwards. By that point in the research, I had temporarily stopped 'noticing' the striking sight of mostly young, wealthy white international intervention staff in expensive cars, hotels and bars. Yet, I reflected, seeing Mozambicans in such places always occasioned me to wonder about the origins of their wealth. Primed by newspaper scandals and anti-corruption reports, I speculated about the nefarious ways in which they might have achieved their positions. But what was the difference, really? Why was it normal for interveners to live this way but not for anyone else? And what was the lesson about wealth and corruption that was being taught by intervention?

International statebuilding interventions are fundamentally – almost by definition – characterised by a concern with the nature of 'governance' in the global South. As seen in chapter 4, one significant aspect of this has been a concern with 'capacity-building' at the level of state institutions.

However, another central pillar of 'good governance' activity has become 'anti-corruption' efforts. This has led to a proliferation of donor intervention strategies based on 'an international consensus [that] has now emerged that corruption and poor governance fuel state failure, deter foreign investment, and cripple economic growth and development' (USAID 2005: v). Based on the power of this consensus, good governance *qua* anti-corruption has become one of the most prominent and well-funded aspects of international intervention, spawning a wide array of strategies, forums, conferences, grants, working groups, government agencies and advisers, and increasingly integrated as a form of conditionality into wider transformation efforts (Doornbos 2001).

In order to 'decolonise' our understanding of these issues, it is necessary, as argued in chapter 3, to root such an understanding outside the discourses of intervention, and instead within a sense of the historical presence, political consciousness and material conditions of those people targeted by such programmes. As this chapter shows, international intervention efforts are a real but relatively limited part of anti-corruption politics within Mozambique, which has much deeper historical roots and addresses a broader set of political and moral problems than those identified by good governance strategies. Moreover, it encompasses not only the behaviour of political elites and citizens but also that of interveners and the system generated by intervention itself, as indicated in the opening of this chapter. The chapter traces three forms of discourse that contribute to the politics of anti-corruption in Mozambique – the promotion of 'good governance', the memorialisation of Samora Machel, and the fears of insatiable, unknowable greed. This wide and varied landscape locates the problem of corruption *beyond* the legality and transparency of conduct with which intervention is concerned, and within a broader critique of the changes in society since the end of the war.

GOOD GOVERNANCE AND THE
PROSPECT OF RADICAL CRITIQUE

The move towards the goal of 'good governance' in shaping international aid flows and development agendas as part of a 'liberal' transformation agenda has been in the gradual process of institutionalisation for around two decades. As such, 'good governance' demands are thus viewed in much of the critical literature as a key site of deep Western intrusion into the social and political orders of aid-recipient countries (Williams 2008). In particular, these are seen to be aligned with concerns to make countries fit for foreign investment through the reduction of risks and instability (Wei 2001).

Alongside many other countries, Mozambique was targeted by a number of intervener funds and strategies designed to fight corruption. These included funds to reform the public sector financial management systems as well as funds to civil society organisations concerned with questions of good governance and anti-corruption. Many of these organisations have performed their functions in a way which appears to have satisfied their external funders – indeed the multiple extension of funding arrangements for these organisations indicates their success in this regard. Journalists within Mozambique have also participated within these organisations and developed expertise on 'good governance' issues.

However, to frame this engagement as simply capitulation to an external liberal framework or the internal 'hand' of interveners does not capture the ways in which such organisations and writers have often gone far beyond a generic 'good governance' agenda. Rather, they have used and reconfigured the ideas as a form of immanent critical consciousness towards the existing political order, as well as a challenge to the character of foreign intervention and investment. In short, they have embraced the wider consequences of an anti-corruption platform under a 'good governance' regime. As Noe Nhantumbo, a journalist, writes in a recent book:

> the most important thing is that the political forces of civil society know how to take advantage of this genuine 'external aid', and make the 'Good Governance' question their own, taking in full and with all its consequences ... To know how to take advantage of and use the small open windows for the evolution and growth of international political relations is a necessity ... It is in this way that we must look at the issue of 'Good Governance'. The risk that we currently run is to view this issue as being appropriated by politicians and leaders, to be later sold to the international community when they invite them. (Nhantumbo 2007: 100–101)

Some outlets have been attempting to use these 'small open windows' as a way to develop a critical account of power. By way of example, one of the currently most prominent and best-funded NGOs for 'good governance' in Mozambique is the *Centro de Integridade Pública* (CIP) run by Marcelo Mosse, an investigative journalist and public commentator, and Adriano Nuvunga, a lecturer at Eduardo Mondlane University, and funded by Denmark, the Netherlands, Sweden, Switzerland, the United Kingdom, Norway, the Ford Foundation and International Budget Partnership.[2] Much of the work of the centre is given over to the monitoring and advocacy of corruption and governance issues, the provision of training and the evaluation of the effectiveness of government policy. Indeed, many of the angles of analysis used to diagnose political problems and corruption are framed in ways which are compatible with a technocratic approach to governance, such as a focus on accountability mechanisms and the implementation of laws (Mosse 2006).

Yet, in many cases, the issues discussed, the quality of investigation and commitment to analysis vastly exceeds efforts made by either government or development partners and is undertaken in an environment where, as previously discussed, lethal violence has been used against those who investigate corruption. In particular, recent analyses of the Extractive Industries and Public Private Partnerships have been extremely specific and vocal in their challenges to specific processes, contracts and tenders. These criticisms not only encompass conflicts of interests amongst the Mozambican political elite, but also implicate companies, international investment vehicles and the international policies which support these practices. In this sense it retains a focus on the idea of 'public integrity' as a *moral* activity as well as a *multidimensional* political problem, rather than primarily a technical one.

This has involved a much broader critique – through the idea of good governance – of how international intervention operates at a structural level in the state. Nuvunga, for example, via a discussion on governance, develops an account of the functioning of the state that corresponds to what was discussed in chapter 4:

> Aid appears to have helped build, but also fragment, the State machinery and institutions. It appears that dependence on aid has created an incentive structure that makes civil servants reluctant to get involved and commit themselves to public duties unless there is a prospect of direct personal benefit in the form of perks. (Nuvunga 2007: 49–50)

He goes on to argue that the movement towards central budget support has in fact led to perverse consequences for 'governance':

> donors not only control national policy through aid conditionality, they also control key institutions through their direct involvement. This has long-term consequences for institutional sustainability in the country. (Nuvunga 2007: 49–50)

Although using the framework of 'good governance', Nuvunga's analysis offers a gently stated if far-reaching structural critique of the role of aid in the political sphere of Mozambique, and one which is directed at the donors as well as the government. This is supplemented by a number of political commentaries co-published regularly with Joe Hanlon, which interrogate the relationship between donors and government closely and underscore the problems of political legitimacy and accountability with it.[3] This interpretation of 'good governance' thus puts emphasis on the specifically *democratic* rather than bureaucratic ways in which the term can be understood, opening up the political space for a different kind of critique. Indeed, donors' own discourses of what constitutes 'good governance' in Mozambique appeared to have changed over the years in line with the diagnoses of activists, including those regarding the dominance of Frelimo in political life. As Hanlon (2004) notes, for a long time there was a deep reluctance by the donors to engage with issues of governance in anything other than a technical fashion.

The idea that the structures of intervention promote governance failure through its own policies is one advocated by Marcelo Mosse, who argues strongly from a good governance platform that cuts in public sector salaries imposed by structural adjustment policies were a major cause of corruption that both the government and donors wanted to ignore (2006). This corroborates with analysis heard elsewhere in interviews and newspaper discussions – that cuts to public sector salaries following structural adjustment were a primary driver of corruption in the post-war environment. Mosse also explains the ways in which the ideological drive for privatisation amongst donors in the early 1990s facilitated corruption – an analysis picked up even now in the state-friendly *Noticias* newspaper.[4]

In this kind of reappropriated 'good governance' consciousness, donors themselves are also accused of failing to uphold 'good governance' in their dealings with the government of Mozambique. Since the Paris Declaration and movement towards aid harmonisation, the government itself has launched a number of audits of bureaucratic delays within the aid system, as mentioned in chapter 4. These have presented findings that the majority of delays in processes were attributable to delays at the World Bank or EU rather than the government, which has been since used to pressure them politically.[5] Others have noted more ironically that despite pressing for legislative reform, donor agencies have undermined the 'good governance' they promote by not following these procurement and employment laws themselves in their own practices (CanalMoz 2009).[6] This is supplemented by the idea that there has also been a failure of governance in donor countries, as noted by another public intellectual:

> The other thing that needs to happen is that European citizens need to ask their governments where the money is going – what are you doing? Because it is going from the taxpayers of Europe – the working people – to the rich of Africa [laughs]. I was asked to give advice to a lady from a Finnish organisation who was working on a poster to raise funds for her organisation. It was a poster of an African child who was hungry. I advised her to add a picture of the politician's mansion across the road. She didn't do it ... but this is what I mean. You have your own internal mechanisms for monitoring ... but you need to go and see.[7]

A political consciousness of 'good governance' in Mozambique can be understood as not one which simply reproduces a technocratic ideology of donor-led development, although it may also do this, but one which also looks at the structure of the political and economic order more broadly and critically through the lenses of inequality and unaccountability. For Nhantumbo, the idea of 'good governance' is amenable to be rescued from 'the deceptive mires of the mouth' as the basis for a much more radical critique of the international order through a more widespread democratisation of power and resources. Yet, he argues that this has implications that neither the politicians of Africa nor the West will embrace:

> On both sides, in Africa and in the West, politicians are using or presenting a version of policy which is double-faced. They know that they need to keep 'Good Governance' as a continued factor and condition of cooperation but they are aware that to take it to its logical conclusions would infallibly destroy the bases on which their economies sit. From here we may gather that the politicians and governors will never sufficiently advance, in the implementation of the totality of this strategy or policy because this will contradict their interests in this domain. Only a change in the fundamental strategies between the partners is what can bring about an open and profound approach to the issue of 'Good Governance'. (2007: 103)

Nhantumbo's analysis ties together the dysfunctions of intervention with the interests of interveners and those of the government. He advocates, however, not for a rejection of international assistance and cooperation but a more radical reappraisal of how it is approached and whose interests it serves. His vision of how Africans might approach and use the idea of 'good governance' illustrates perfectly how a seemingly technocratic and politically innocuous discourse can itself be turned towards a more far-reaching critique of political leadership, the distribution of wealth and international interventions.

Whilst the language of 'good governance' thus has the potential to underpinning a critical political posture, it is not one in which more than a relatively limited number of public figures habitually express themselves, and its own power is somewhat limited. Much more prevalent at a public level are those discourses with resonances with aspects of national identity and collective being. These not only provide a more compelling point of accountability for most Mozambicans but also allow the discussion of a wider set of issues than that permitted by the language of 'good governance'. In the next two sections of the chapter, both the icon of Samora Machel and public discourses about greed are shown to underpin a richer and deeper conception of the ways in which corruption emerges and functions within society.

'ISSO NÃO ACONTECIA SE SAMORA ESTIVESSE VIVO' – 'THIS WOULD NOT BE HAPPENING IF SAMORA WAS ALIVE'[8]

One of the most potent and most common responses to contemporary public corruption scandals in Mozambique is via unfavourable and nostalgic comparison to the political leadership under the first ten years of the post-independence government after 1975, led by President Samora Machel. Although the latter part of this is also commonly known as the *tempo de fome* (time of hunger), it is also memorialised in many circles as a time when public institutions functioned with a keen sense of purpose, transparency and enthusiasm. In particular, Machel was seen to attack vigorously, denounce and severely punish corruption in the public sphere as simultaneously colonialist, immoral and counter-revolutionary (Harrison 1999). Machel's lengthy political discourses, broadcast nationally via the only television and radio channels, elaborated passionately and in detail the distinctions between a corrupt colonialism and the kind of society that Frelimo aimed to build:

> That's what colonialism means: bribery, corruption and immorality; robbery; nepotism, favouritism and patronage; individualism and ambition; servility and subservience ... Destroying all this was the aim of the armed struggle for national liberation. (Machel, cited in Harrison 1999: 540)

Machel's presidency is remembered for the stringent and vigilant punishment of transgressions and corruption in public administration. One famous tactic involved personal unannounced spot checks on various parts of the state machinery across the country, including then state enterprises and farms. Irregularities of any sort would result in public castigation, which would be often followed by summary dismissal.[9] More serious criminal transgressions were punished much more severely, culminating in several public executions. One of the most high-profile of these cases was the execution by firing squad of the prawn merchant Gulam Nabi, who had been bribing customs officials (Hanlon 1984: 208). Moreover, it was made clear that Machel's attitudes to corruption were widely shared – the suicide of Francisco Langa, a Frelimo cadre who had embezzled funds, was publicly attributed to very intense personal shame by the party, who made an example of him (195).

During the 1980s, government propaganda on the theme revolved around the image of 'Xiconhoca' – a character who was seen to collaborate with Portuguese secret agents in the independence struggle but pretended to support the new government, and who was lazy, drunk, corrupt and self-serving. Cartoons, such as that shown in figure 6.1, showed him in a range of situations and roles grotesquely undermining the new, virtuous regime at the level of both practice and ideology in his selfish conduct and orientation. He is described, in the militant idiom of this new order, as 'the enemy'.

'Xiconhoca' was seen to embody a corruption which was as much moral and political as it was material. In this sense, corruption was perceived as an active threat to the programme of radical revolutionary change which Frelimo aspired to bring about in this period. Much of this focused on, and indeed

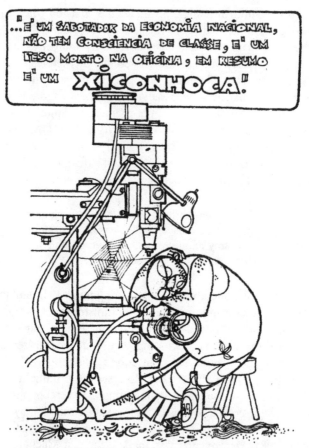

Figure 6.1. *Xiconhoca O Inimigo* (c. 1979: Mozambique History Net, http://www.
mozambiquehistory.net/cartoons.html; Maputo: Frelimo, Edição do Departamento de
Trabalho Ideológico): *'He's a saboteur of the national economy, he has no class consciousness, he's a dead weight in the office, to summarise, he's a Xiconhoca'.*

depended on, the personal conduct of the citizens and their embrace of the
'New Man' ideology elaborated by the party's ideologues. Public education,
which rapidly expanded in the post-independence period, was tasked with the
ongoing formation of 'New Men', who would be literate, technically profi-
cient and morally dedicated to the construction of the Revolution. Those who
were compromised by corrupt or anti-revolutionary behaviour were often dis-
patched to remote provinces to be 're-educated' in drastic and violent ways.

Samora Machel was killed in a plane crash in 1986 in suspicious circumstances, yet his figure looms large in contemporary political consciousness.
This is the case especially amongst younger generations, who have sought to

critique the recent and contemporary political environment through the recovered figure of Samora (Sumich 2007). This recovery of a tradition of moral opposition to corruption has emerged on several different fronts, including within the ruling party, amongst public academic and political commentators in the press, in the political opposition, amongst the urban youth and middle-class, amongst the unions and within the blogosphere. At the core of this consciousness is a narrative of Mozambican moral rectitude, transparency and decisiveness which Samora is seen to embody.

The reclamation of Machel's legacy as a form of political consciousness takes place in a political context of visible corruption and increasing inequality, for which the context is the structural reform of the economy through IMF conditionality, the end of the war, and the vast influx in aid money both in response to famine and in the period after the war. Under Joaquim Chissano's leadership, Mozambique was opened up economically and politically, and aid money flooded in. For various reasons, including the context of emergency and the lack of oversight, much of this money and these resources were never accounted for, according to multiple interviewees. Mozambique nonetheless became a prominent 'donor darling' on the international scene, broadly endorsed for its wise post-war political and economic choices and strong growth rates, forgiven much public debt and made the recipient of one of the highest per capita aid flows of sub-Saharan Africa.

This coincided with a visible change in the wealth of elites, particularly those in and connected to the Frelimo party. This change was linked in part to the effect of donor money and policy on liberalisation and privatisation (Harrison 1999; Pitcher 2002; Hanlon 2004). During this period, various corruption scandals emerged regarding thefts and embezzlements from former state enterprises, which were of widespread public knowledge and disquiet. The most notorious of these related to the banking sector, during the course of which the country's leading investigative journalist, Carlos Cardoso, and the interim director of banking supervision, Siba-Siba Macuacua, were murdered. Those implicated in the murder included a number of the Presidential Guard as well as Chissano's son Nyimpine, whose testimonies in the trial were televised (Sumich 2007; Hanlon 2003). This episode accelerated what had been an increasing level of political dissatisfaction with the perceived *deixa andar* (let it go) attitude of Chissano regarding the widespread criminality and corruption in the state at all levels. Chissano's decreasing public popularity could already be seen in the results of the 1999 presidential election, which resulted in only a narrow victory under rather dubious circumstances.

Within the Frelimo party this consciousness emerged from what was then Armando Guebuza's faction, who claimed the inheritance of Machel's mantle. They claimed this legacy in the run-up to the 2004 presidential election, when Chissano's administration was criticised for its *deixa andar* approach

(Mosse 2004: 81). As Hanlon reports, after winning the election, Guebuza's administration from 2005 visibly reactivated many of the political discourses, practices and habits of Machel, including unannounced spot checks in public institutions and services (2005: 2). Guebuza's administration also took care to celebrate Machel publicly, including building striking new monuments to him around the country and declaring 2011 Samora Machel Year.

Guebuza's narrative of his own moral, Machel-like stand on corruption was sold to, but not entirely bought by, a wide range of audiences, who have continued to use Samora and the socialist legacy as a political resource in critiquing corruption within contemporary Frelimo as well as the effects of Mozambique's liberalisation. It is perhaps unremarkable to note that this has been a feature of internal Frelimo struggles, particularly in factions associated with Samora's widow Graça Machel, who argued that honest people had been excluded from the government in order for corruption to continue (Mabunda 2010).

But this line of argument has also been a feature of the more independent press. Even as Guebuza promised to restore a sense of morality in the state, he was accused of doing so only in speeches but not in practice by journalists such as Machado da Graça, who argued that, unlike Samora, he lacked the political will to do so (Mucavele 2005). Indeed, during his presidency, it was reported that Guebuza was also the wealthiest person in Mozambique. Borges Nhamirre, a commentator on *CanalMoz*, has also pointed out that under Samora the salaries of high-ranking state officials were fixed by law, were public knowledge and that perks of the job were not permitted, in clear distinction to today's practices (Nhamirre 2011). These are commentators who occupy different parts of the political spectrum and speak outside the Frelimo party but who engage in the recovery of Samora as part of a critical and broadly salient form of political consciousness.

Perhaps more surprising is the resurrection of Samora by an opposition whose members waged open warfare against Samora's government in the 1980s. In a recent TV debate on the political thought of Samora Machel – the holding of which is perhaps in and of itself revealing – Máximo Días, a former Renamo deputy, argued that if Samora were alive, many of today's leaders would be in jail for their failure to uphold transparency.

> According to him, 'some have the understanding that I have already liberated the country, and now I must liberate myself from myself', and each takes his own decision to enrich himself. (Banze 2011)

At this same debate, he asked for financial contributions for a Samora Machel Academy, which would be dedicated to 'the promotion of the ideas of Samora Machel, namely: the fight against corruption, transparency, amongst other virtues the remains of which are in question today'. Whilst the sincerity of this resurrection by the opposition is questioned, particularly by a sceptical public spotting opportunism,[10] it is clear that its political resonance in terms of public consciousness is real in terms of the critique of profiteering offered.

Yet, perhaps tellingly, the idea of Samora's era as an uncorrupt one is particularly visible as a form of political consciousness amongst the urban youth who were not yet born during his rule. This group, as Sumich notes, some of whom have taken to wearing T-shirts bearing Samora's image, tends to speak favourably of this more equal, more honest time (2007: 13). Across my own discussions this was a repeated theme – that under Samora these sorts of transgressions did not occur and that people worked for the public good.[11] This critique is also borne out in various aspects of popular culture. As an example, the popular MC Azagaia, Edson da Luz, has interspersed clips of Samora's speeches against corruption into his music videos, in which his own lyrics condemn the 'liberators' of Mozambique – that is, the ruling Frelimo elite – as mere mercenaries, enriching themselves, lacking ideology and selling images of hunger to make a profit. In the closing frames of the video, Samora is shown giving a public address, saying, 'We cannot build happiness or well-being with bandits and thieves ... Correct? But it must be you who dislodge the bandits and thieves. Denounce them. Kick them out' (Azagaia 2009).

The icon of Samora as a symbol of political honesty and purpose thus continues to occupy a dominant role in public debates on corruption in a way which ties together the central co-ordinates of Mozambican nationalism as being about the legacies of anti-colonial liberation with the present situation of sharply increased inequality and enormous wealth at the level of elites. This is visible even where the government is pursuing the anti-corruption strategies encouraged by donors. We see an example of this in the recent establishment of the Gabinete Central de Combate a Corrupção (GCCC), which formed a key pillar of its 'good governance' strategy, which itself occasioned the release of aid monies. At the opening of its new Chinese-funded headquarters, in which its main meeting room was named after Samora, its director, Ana Maria Gemo, argued

that Samora Machel fought corruption vehemently and advocated an equitable distribution of national wealth. 'He dedicated his life to the building of a fair and transparent public administration, whether through creating legal instruments, or otherwise in his vigorous speeches, teaching Mozambicans to be determined and persistent regarding obstacles to any development of our young nation ... *in following the teachings of Samora, in this room, we will develop strategies for crime prevention, civic education, which are aimed at promoting citizenship, a culture of transparency, integrity and good governance.* Strategies will be aligned to the establishment of trust in institutions of public administration and justice, because, after all, corruption is a challenge within our grasp'. (O País 2011; emphasis added)

The multiple ways in which the legacy of Samora has been appropriated in the recent past speaks to its power and significance within Mozambican society, particularly at the level of popular discourse. Within these debates, we already see ways in which such a legacy serves as a rich point of reference for an anti-corruption politics which is expansive, resonates with a founding political identity and articulates a particular ethic of public service which is sensed to have been lost. Although the complaint – that things would not be like this if Samora was alive – is also occasionally mocked as *saudadista* (a kind of wistful nostalgic orientation), it is nonetheless one which pierces his would-be successors at the heart of one of their claims to political legitimacy.

The icon of Samora speaks to the question of corruption as emerging out of selfishness, a lack of collective loyalty, a lack of personal integrity and a lack of sense of public service. In this discourse, to talk about corruption is to talk about the ways in which members of society and the government are *motivated* in their conduct, as well as the subsequent distribution of national wealth that results from their decisions. This already greatly transcends the ideas of good governance as transparency by requiring a form of moral judgement or accountability to the collective – and much enrichment by political elites for example happens very transparently at any rate. By resurrecting Samora, Mozambicans challenge the kinds of changes to society that have been happening since the end of the war and particularly the production of inequalities since the turn to a more liberal market capitalism.

However, *saudades* for Samora are not the only form of political consciousness responding to the issues of corruption and governance. In articulating a deeper politics of anti-corruption, many Mozambicans attack the question of greed directly as a function of uncontrolled and unseemly appetites, and sometimes worked through occult means. These ideas again build towards an explanation and critique of the root causes of corruption as being moral and political rather than technical.

BLOODSUCKING, GREED AND POWER

A satirical play was put on in Maputo, Mozambique's capital, in July 2009. Entitled *The Politics of the Belly* and written by the youth theatre group who staged it, the narrative followed the adventures of a teenager as he sought to tell the difference between lies and truth within contemporary Mozambican society. In a series of hilarious encounters with his father, the school, the police, some drunken army veterans, a nightclub owner and the national parliament, the young man's naïve questions expose the hypocrisies, cruelties and absurdities at the heart of various claims to authority in his life.[12] The actors, many of whom were university students, were well acquainted with

Jean-François Bayart's (1993 [1989]) opus of the same name on the nature of the African state. Yet, within the plot and narrative, they were also trading on a wider public sensibility of the politics of corruption as a social crisis of appetite, greed and dishonesty.

Within public discourse, the figure of the *cabrito* or goat is emblematic of this idea. The *cabrito* is a widely recognised representation of a corrupt public official – one who is greedy, mindless and seeks to profit from his/her immediate surroundings. Like the *Xiconhoca* character, the *cabrito* has also appeared in many public anti-corruption campaigns and cartoons, taking bribes in public offices and services and undermining efforts for development. The term *cabritismo* is used liberally in media discussions of corruption, capturing a level of disgust and derision towards these practices, as well as an understanding of how pervasive they have become. Such complaints are in part tied to a sense of government failures to tackle corruption – more than one interviewee recalled former president Chissano's *deixa andar* (i.e. *laissez-faire*) attitude and reported his dismissive response to complaints with considerable indignation – 'goats eat where they are tied'. Mozambican writer Mia Couto popularised the term *cabritalismo* as a way of capturing the relationship of the turn to capitalism and the emergence of widespread *cabritismo,* which enabled officials to eat according to the length of their rope (i.e. their seniority/responsibility) (Harrison 1999: 548).

However, the idea of corruption as wanton, greedy consumption also draws connections back to wider understandings of the uses of sorcery and black magic to enable certain individuals – almost always outsiders to a community – to drain power/life from others and advance their status or projects. In particular, fears of the *chupa-sangue* (bloodsucker or vampire) are relatively common in different parts of the country – for example, in 2015 a number of urban *bairros* in Nampula experienced the terror of a *chupa-sangue* attack that led to nocturnal vigils and some families choosing to sleep in the bush at night (Savana 2015). This was explained by one resident as directly a fear that the 'procuring of blood was to guarantee that the government had money, since when Nyusi took charge the coffers were empty' (Savana 2015).

Mozambican sociologist Carlos Serra traces the emergence of the *chupa-sangue* rumours in the postcolonial era as being first associated with Frelimo's *Grupos Dinamizadores* (GDs) in 1975 in Zambezia. GDs were detachments of party activists sent to modernise communities and ensure their loyalty, but rumours spread that they were vampires who had come to suck the blood of the communities in order to manufacture money for the new country and to support its hospitals (Serra 2015). The rumours were reattached to the Red Cross in the late 1980s when they advertised for blood donors, and with the presence of outsiders during outbreaks of cholera, malaria and meningitis. In each of these cases, the weakness and illness within the community is associated with predatory outsiders who have come to deplete their strength and resources.

Elsewhere, there are contexts in which this broader fear of predation also manifests as a questioning of the accumulation of power and wealth. In extended studies of peoples on the Muedan plateau in northern Mozambique, West (2005, 2008a, 2008b) presents sorcery as one such hermeneutic of governance. In Mueda, it is believed amongst the Makonde that sorcerers are highly powerful and accumulate this power through the means of *uwavi* – a knowledge and mastery over the invisible realm, often but not always used for malevolent ends. Practitioners of *uwavi* are said to maintain their power through feasting on human flesh, through deploying invisible helicopters and planes to bomb their enemies, through turning themselves into lions and through holding zombified slaves. In order to counteract the power of sorcerers, ordinary Muedans practice different forms of *kupilikula* – protective counter-sorcery rites – many of which rely on using natural and man-made objects invested with spiritual power (*mitela*). However, few profess knowledge of *uwavi* itself – rather, it is held to be broadly mysterious except to its alleged practitioners (West 2005).

Discourses of *uwavi* and *kupilikula* interact in multiple ways with the structures of political power on the plateau. 'Big chiefs' in the villages, in the Frelimo government, and their associates have been long believed to exercise forms of sorcery in the conduct of their affairs, both for the means of protecting the population and, increasingly, for self-enrichment. As such, the common representation of leaders as 'eating everything', 'eating alone' or having large appetites can be understood to refer simultaneously to their control over material goods and their appetite to consume flesh to make them more powerful (West 2005: 180–189). West further argues that the advent of privatisation and the sudden and mysterious accumulation of wealth by various parties has been interpreted in Mueda as likely involving practices of *uwavi*, particularly the use of zombie-slaves (186).

Examining West's descriptions of the ways in which *uwavi* is discussed, it is *uncontrolled greed itself*, and the fear and envy it generates, that is seen as potentially damaging, 'anti-social' and in need of policing (2005: 35–37). We can contrast this sensibility with the notion of 'corruption' expressed in 'good governance' discourse, which differentiates only between 'legal' and 'illegal' forms of enrichment. Whilst this seems to resonate more closely with the nostalgic discourses about socialist purity in endorsing a collectivist ethos towards the distribution of social goods, consciousness of *uwavi* also captures a sensibility about the double-edged nature of protection/predation, as well as the temptations that draw people towards *uwavi*.

Moreover, West argues that the framing of *uwavi* draws attention to the specifically unpredictable and non-transparent ways in which power is harnessed and deployed, meaning that many ordinary Muedans feel subject to its force but unable to intervene in the effects it produces. This is particularly pertinent to the ways in which the advent of democracy on the plateau was received – in which the wielding of power was meant to have been rendered transparent and accountable (2005: 265–266). Instead, the period of democratic decentralisation and associated privatisation in Mueda has been interpreted as effective *abandonment* by the state, leading to increased reports of *uwavi* and attacks on its alleged practitioners (West and Kloeck-Jenson 1999; West 2008a).

Fears and rumours of the *chupa-sangue* and practices of *kupilikula* are also connected to understandings of colonialism in Mozambique. Specifically, these include the beliefs in parts of Mozambique that the Portuguese colonisers were themselves vampires/bloodsuckers who had come to feast on the flesh of Africans (Pimentel Teixeira 2003). In discussing *kupilikula* practices in colonial times, West reports a social dynamic intended to contain the effects of a greedy and voracious colonial power: 'The *régulo* ate the people. And the Portuguese ate the *régulo*' (2008: 99). And yet, in the Muedan accounts, this is always bound up with the consumption and appetites of those amongst themselves – those who encouraged and profited from the presence of outsiders, leaving them to abandon their people.

In anti-corruption politics in Mozambique, the invocation of ideas of greedy bloodsucking by powerful figures in the public eye is thus not a metaphorical whimsy or one derived from exposure to popular Western representations of vampires. Rather, it is steeped in a public hermeneutic of what it means to consume and control, particularly through a targeting of those who work hardest. When challenged during his 2009 electoral campaign about the problems of corruption, the then president Guebuza exclaimed, to a standing ovation, that

'to promote corruption, in the State or in the private sector, is the same as "drinking or even sucking" the blood of a brother'. Speaking today, in a grand public rally taking place in the municipality of Manica, Guebuza said that even now promoters of corruption spend a lot of time coveting the few means of those who sweat night and day to earn a living. (O País 2009)

Yet, and as seen with other forms of anti-corruption consciousness earlier, this discourse is also turned back on those that wield it. In attacking the reported decision of the government to authorise the purchase of luxury cars despite a recent public financial crisis, Machado de Graça enters full declamatory mode:

At a time when we are expecting from the Government a proposal to cut costs and measures to curb inflation, the apes – pardon, the rulers of this country – do the opposite: they are worried about going to the tailor to increase the size of

their trousers and jackets, due to the huge growth of their bellies at the expense
of our taxes … In fact, the leaders we have today are a real public danger, that
is, they are political vampires who suffer at the expense of the suffering and
widespread underdevelopment of Mozambicans. Drowned in massive lunches
and dinners, washed down with wine and whiskey, tightened in Italian suits and
accommodated in luxury cars paid for with the blood, sweat and tears of the
people, they contribute, in the Government, to take the country to the abyss.
(@Verdade 2016)

For many within Mozambique, then, understandings of corruption are
inseparable from a moral and political discourse about consumption, greed
and voracity, which is entangled with a relational sensibility about who gets
rich at the expense of whom. The *cabrito* and the *chupa-sangue* are *inhuman*
public menaces who will eat everything up, drain you of your own life force,
grow fat at your expense and put you to work for them. In a recent context
where politics and intervention have been supposedly oriented around the
alleviation of poverty through economic liberalisation – and in colonial
and socialist times around the civilisation or development of society – the
ongoing presence of such figures is a testament to the predatory dynamics
embedded within such projects. Such dynamics of self-enrichment are also
understood as internal to the intervention project itself. In the next section,
reflections on corruption which also incorporated critiques of intervention are
discussed, showing that it too forms part of the moral and political universe
under scrutiny.

ANTI-CORRUPTION AND INTERVENTION

In an interview with a Mozambican agronomist who had worked for a
long time in the international aid industry, our conversation turned to the
meaning of corruption. As an example, he spoke about the costs spent on
international assistance projects in keeping workers in cars and houses. He
says he knew a Norwegian project, which was something like 3.5 million
euros, which had ten expensive cars. As another example, he says that he
knows a couple, who run an HIV/AIDS organisation in Maputo, whose
place is worth US$7,000 per month. '*So what is corruption? Who are the
criminals?*'[13]

It is of course widely known that expatriate staff costs and salaries are – in
relative terms to the public – extremely high in Mozambique. Indeed, the
luxurious conditions of aid workers are now a highly visible and universal
cultural cliché of the contemporary aid environment (Smirl 2015). Pfeiffer
summarises conditions in the post-war health sector in Mozambique for many
expatriates:

With the exception of two agencies, expatriates were paid from US$1000 to US$6000 per month, usually tax-free. Most agencies provided housing, private access to project cars, and funding for personal vacations. One engineer working for a European agency calculated that at the end of his four-year contract he would have saved nearly US$300,000. (Pfeiffer 2003: 730)[14]

In project-based assistance, costs associated with supporting expatriates through salaries, housing and transport can consume up to 50 per cent of the budget, although in programme aid it is likely to be less. In other cases, it can be more, which was the cause of some consternation to interviewees:

we thought of discussing the budget: where does the budget go to? You can't! You don't know. The way it's written, it's written in such a way that you can't see where things go, and this has been a struggle to make it more clear so that it can be analysed by people ... If I tell you that I had a project in Zambezia where we were giving $150,000 of social security funds to communities, and *we spent $1 million to do that* ... these were the things that I couldn't agree in the NGO.[15]

This spending has a knock-on effect in terms of the conditions in the public sector, where *cabritismo* is understood to be rife. Rentals in the neighbourhoods in Maputo where expatriate workers generally live are high, pushed up by the large numbers of aid workers and their respective housing allowances (Hanlon 1996; interviews), which have pushed up demand elsewhere. As an example, the US State Department's published 2011 housing allowance for each worker based in Maputo was between US$28,700 and US$39,500 per year (US State Department 2011b).[16] For temporary visiting staff in Mozambique, there was a per diem allowance of up to US$238 for hotels and accommodation in Maputo and US$220 elsewhere (US State Department 2011c). Salaries, beginning at US$27,431, rising to US$129,517, were also subject to a 25 per cent hardship boost and a 35 per cent cost of living allowance (US State Department 2011a). Published data on UN pay scales indicates similar levels of pay and benefits (International Civil Service Commission 2011). This compares to a 2010 national average annual income of US$410 in Mozambique, or US$34 per month (World Bank 2011). The average annual income in Maputo City in this period could, however, have been over ten times higher (US$1,109) than in the poorest provinces (US$96), where the majority are well below the international poverty line (UNDP Mozambique 2008). A doctor working for the government in this period could expect to receive US$330 per month, which works out as US$3,960 per year (Ferrinho et al. 2011: 9). In this light, the 'brain drain' detailed in chapter 4 can itself be understood as in part a direct consequence of the high status in which expatriates expect to live. These raise the costs of even a moderate standard of living at a reasonable proximity to a workplace, for which many turn to *cabritismo* if they have not left the public sector altogether. As the respondent quoted at the beginning of this chapter asks, 'between you and me, what's the difference'? Why is it that expatriates are seen as *intrinsically entitled* to a better standard of living than Mozambicans?

Other linkages were made between international intervention and corruption of which two are notable. The first is the uncontrolled way in which aid was practised in the immediate aftermath of war, which generated conditions in which self-interest could flourish:

> So, the staff were relaxed, receiving money, receiving meals, but not preparing the state to manage things. They were managing the donations, and not the state, and not working in the interests of the people. This is where the question of corruption emerged – because people came in, no one was controlling anything, and even the donors were not controlling anything, and people began to think of themselves first and how to guarantee their lives.[17]

The sensibility that the flood of donations and donors in the post-war environment had enabled a loss of control and virtue was shared across multiple interviewees, including many who had been directly involved in their disbursement.

The other linkage speaks more directly to how particular contracting practices such as non-transparent tenders were themselves normalised by interveners in ways which are now criticised as corrupt amongst the ruling elites:

> One thing that happened at the time was all these regulations from World Bank, procurements, things like that. When you read, it's very nice; in practice they really taught people how to rob. I said this in a meeting and someone told me 'You won't be allowed to go to the States anymore' [laughter]. I said okay. But I believe the first ones to teach our institutions to rob in procurement and things like that, the World Bank were the first ones to teach this, and they brought all their consultants to organise the procurement units here, and then we discover that these procurement units are all … are fake! They managed their way around … we were not used to it, so before the '80s, probably until very late '80s, Mozambique was a country where you wouldn't think of bribery, of things like that, and so it was a surprise for everybody to see Mozambicans acting like that. It was a shock.[18]

In summary, international interveners, rather than exemplars of public virtue and transparency who can lead anti-corruption efforts, are thus themselves also heavily implicated in the wider project of self-interest and enrichment that underpins anti-corruption politics across Mozambique. Scandal, rumour and unrest attaches to each site of accumulation, and each is suspected of occlusion, manipulation and immorality. Interveners also take care to provide for themselves richly in terms of salaries and conditions of living and working, in a way which underscores a hierarchical binary of entitlement to the fruits of aid. Understood in the light of historic projects of rule and the startling wealth differentials that have accompanied it, international intervention has demonstrated an inability to transcend such dynamics – rather, the perception is that it has accelerated and facilitated unseemly accumulation and greed. Why, then, should it be positioned to lead a fight against it?

***

Decolonising our understanding of corruption – through rooting it in historical forms of political consciousness and material realities – is generative of a wide and rich comprehension of the dynamics which facilitate and sustain it, as well as its moral and political implications. Such a comprehension clearly demonstrates the limits of the liberal-technocratic approach of the interveners, which only manages to distinguish between legal and illegal means of self-enrichment amongst Mozambican public officials. For many Mozambicans, corruption cannot be separated from greed, consumption and capitalist strategies of accumulation, for which international intervention has played an enabling role, and in which almost everyone is implicated. Yet, these hermeneutics also contain other possibilities for society, rooted in better pasts, presents and futures in which such dynamics are not dominant. Can such a decolonising approach help us rethink the politics of intervention from the ground up? Drawing on the experiences of Mozambique, it is to this question that the concluding chapter turns.

NOTES

1. Interview with former agricultural technician working for European donor agency, Sofala, 16 July 2009.

2. *Centro de Integridade Pública* website: http://www.cip.org.mz. Accessed 27 May 2011. It is of note, though, that as a guerrilla group Frelimo itself also started with a grant from the Ford Foundation in the 1960s, solicited by Eduardo Mondlane.

3. See Mozambique Political Process Bulletin, also published at http://www.cip.org.mz.

4. See Maússe and Mabunda (2015, 26 June).

5. Interview with vice-minister of Planning and Development, Maputo, 19 August 2009.

6. Interview with senior civil servant, Ministry of Planning and Development, Maputo, 24 August 2009.

7. Interview with director of good governance NGO, Maputo, 17 August 2009.

8. Popular saying in Maputo. Heard in my own research, also discussed in Sumich (2007: 13).

9. Diary notes of conversation with young hostel worker, 10 June 2009; also Hanlon (2005).

10. Which the below-the-line comments to this particular article clearly show.

11. Diary notes of conversation with hostel worker, Maputo, 10 June 2009; diary notes of conversation with musician, Maputo, 7 July 2008.

12. Teatro Luarte (2009), *The Politics of the Belly*. Performed at Teatro Avenida, Maputo, August 2009.

13. Interview with NGO employee, Nampula, 10 August 2009.

14. Of course, there are variations in this package between permanent, consultant and volunteer staff (McWha 2011), the ability of various organisations to pay salaries, and there is increasing awareness within the aid community about the use of project or programme funds as personal subsidies. Nonetheless, there is a relatively common standard of remuneration, and of living, which is often in excess of what these workers would be able to achieve in their countries of origin.

15. Interview with former public official, Maputo, 12 August 2014.

16. It is not insignificant that the landlords of these properties are often themselves high-ranking members of the ruling party.

17. Interview with NGO worker, Nampula, 1 August 2014.

18. Interview with former public official, Maputo, 12 August 2014.

Chapter Seven

Conclusions

Decolonising Intervention, Decolonising International Relations

We cannot adequately study *any* kind of politics by only thinking with or about the powerful parties. For a standpoint theory tradition this is a form of 'pseudo-objectivity' which ultimately naturalises the subordinate status of the disempowered. In this study, I have sought to cultivate a sense of how international statebuilding is understood by its intended targets, precisely in order to contribute to a better, more holistic understanding of how world politics works. This has implications for how practices are themselves organised.

The wager of the book has been that a 'decolonising' approach (as outlined in chapter 3) would help to combat the Eurocentric tendencies of the scholarly literature (identified in chapter 2), by delivering a fuller account of the political dynamics and significance of intervention (elaborated in chapters 4, 5 and 6). This decolonising approach roots itself in the historical presence, political consciousness and material realities of the targets of intervention, which works to counteract their erasure or reductive representations in more Eurocentric accounts. We have seen through the later chapters of the book that this opens up different aspects of intervention to a deep critical interrogation rooted in the experiences, ideas and histories of the targets of intervention.

In this concluding discussion, I recap the findings from Mozambique and argue that the hermeneutics derived from the decolonising approach support an alternative structural explanation of international intervention as constituted by a global politics of coloniality and relations of colonial difference. Such an explanation renders the dynamics of *protagonismo*, disposability, entitlement and dependency experienced by its targets intelligible. I argue that this framing represents an important analytic departure from the primary existing interpretations of intervention. I go on to discuss ways in which a decolonising approach to the political ethics of intervention suggests the need to fundamentally reframe its political stakes along the lines of responsibility, justice and reparation, whilst suggesting some interim measures for more solidaristic political action in the present.

WHAT HAVE WE LEARNED ABOUT INTERNATIONAL STATEBUILDING? *PROTAGONISMO*, DISPOSABILITY, ENTITLEMENT AND DEPENDENCY

When viewed in a long-term perspective from the site of intervention, the research question 'why does intervention fail?' becomes 'why does intervention *keep failing*?' In our examination of the dynamics of intervention in Mozambique from the perspectives of the targets, the following patterns emerge as worthy of explanation:

First, as shown in chapter 4, international intervention systematically fragments statebuilding efforts – that is, the attempt to consolidate a political and bureaucratic infrastructure that can deliver, with authority and legitimacy, an organised range of public services to its citizens. It does this through a persistent drain on the human and financial resources to the state, even as it aims to supply them, a frequent switching of priorities depending on external trends and initiatives and a lack of flexibility in its forms of assistance. These dynamics of fragmentation have the effect of alienating many state employees from their work and incentivising them to abandon the state, with the knock-on effects of the loss of expertise, institutional memory and accumulated experience. It consumes the resources and energies of those who remain, in the name of a supposed 'capacity-building' that rarely improves state capacities. It also negatively impacts the interactions of citizens and the state, because public services themselves become erratic, unpredictable and unreliable. Significantly, conscious efforts by both the host state and donors to promote 'local ownership' to arrest or reverse these tendencies – exemplified by the Paris Declaration on Aid Effectiveness or the Kaya Kwanga Agreement – have not resulted in broad success. Rather, these dynamics of fragmentation have continued *in spite of* widespread knowledge and understanding of their detrimental effects.

Second, as shown in chapter 5, international interventions have not had strong effects in terms of raising the well-being of the rural poor, despite this being a major source of its claims to legitimacy. Although life is better since the end of the war, and some target groups have managed to realise short-term benefits from participating in development programmes, in other cases, they have been ignored, made unfulfilled promises to and exposed to serious risks, especially the poorer people. Moreover, some of these programmes and policies have detracted from the state's ability or willingness to consolidate a broad supportive national infrastructure for agricultural production and rural economic development. This is despite substantive investment in an intellectual infrastructure that points to the need to do so and resources intended to consolidate state capacity. The state, itself increasingly fragmented on this point, has instead been 'punished' by donors for pursuing alternative policies through the withdrawal of major sources of prospective funding for the sector. In this sense, some of the larger interveners are clearly *more committed to having things done their way* than they are to supporting the state in general as a vehicle of public service delivery or economic uplift.

Third, as shown in chapter 6, interveners are not themselves necessarily understood to be harbingers of a less corrupt politics, although they have provided some important support in this regard for some actors. Nonetheless, the technocratic 'good governance' approach to corruption promoted by intervention is itself inadequate for grasping its political and distributive significance, specifically in the context of the 'savage capitalism' (Mosca 2011: 444) that has emerged since the end of the war. A wider and richer public consciousness on the issue of corruption locates these in the coarticulations of greed, power, entitlement and the capacity to hide one's actions. This critique is primarily directed at the country's political elites and public servants for enriching themselves through their access to power; yet it is also one in which international intervention is itself co-implicated as historical cause, ongoing enabler and exemplar.

Viewed in the light of these dynamics drawn from the interpretations and experiences of the targets, international intervention appears lumbering, demanding, hypocritical, narcissistic, limited and irresponsible. How can we make sense of this as a *political* phenomenon? Thinking with the standpoint of its targets, four structural features come into view.

First, the dynamic of *protagonismo*, identified by respondents, attributes to donors a kind of political need to insert oneself into the narrative and feel one's influence in any particular policy sector to feel it is worthwhile. Indeed, this corresponds to reports that donors have pulled out of sectors where they feel their influence is diminishing, leading to a reduction in the proportion of aid in that sector directed through the target state. It may be one way of explaining why donors retain bilateral aid programmes despite also contributing to multiple regional and multilateral funds. This need for *protagonismo* is not reducible to 'vested interests', nor does it correspond to a consistent attachment to specific liberal ideological prerogatives; rather, it appears to be a structural political need for presence, effect and significance over and above this. Colloquially, it might be glossed as the 'ego' of intervention, although this does not quite capture its relational and dynamic qualities in the context of co-operation. It should be noted that this is not a criticism of individual attitudes of 'superiority' but a structural dynamic which consistently constrains attempts to cede any real 'ownership' to the targets of intervention.

As an explanatory concept, *protagonismo* captures a key dynamic in the aid relationship hitherto not discussed as a cause of structural failure in the literature.

Second, and relatedly, there is a strong sense of the relative disposability of the target state and society compared to the interveners.[1] Specifically, the repeated failures and experiments within intervention are not understood by the donors to have any opportunity costs in terms of time or engagement for the counterpart or beneficiaries, so – apart from the financial cost borne by the donor – the failures of intervention are treated as relatively costless. This is because for the most part the targets of intervention – elite and other – are treated as people without histories or ideas, or ongoing other activities – in other words, as blank slates. Yet, rather obviously once one thinks from the bottom up, intervention has very clear costs for its targets in terms of time and lost energies within activities which most likely have no long-term impact because they are inadequately designed, resourced, scheduled or followed up.

The practice of incentivising people to show up with generous *per diems* or other benefits means that attention is diverted from the wider costs and value of the programme itself when trying to engage the targets of intervention. Indeed, the demand for a *per diem* payment can be understood as resistance to the wider politics of disposability in which 'beneficiaries' are otherwise interpellated. Even if donor employees do not believe that there is no cost to failure privately, publicly there is no accounting for or acceptance of responsibility or cost for failed action, particularly outside the immediate life cycle of a project or programme. This is *despite* an extensive and expensive 'monitoring and evaluation' infrastructure within international co-operation, which is constantly trying to measure the 'impact' of aid.

This politics of disposability for the beneficiaries is married to the third feature, a relative politics of entitlement amongst the interveners, as demonstrated through the dynamics of how interveners themselves are rewarded and looked after. Entitlement is a political relation of which inequality is the descriptive outcome – it is a set of presumptions endowing certain parties with the right to a particular set of privileges. A system of valuing, insuring and rewarding interveners very far over and above people in the target country not only has the clear political implication that they are particularly special human beings compared to everyone else, but it even suggests the interpretation that the primary purpose of intervention is to provide for their political presence, comfort and luxurious lifestyles. Their collective presence in turn reorients the structural conditions of living for those working within the state, who must negotiate this politics of entitlement in order to attempt to live in comparable levels of comfort and safety and provide for their families. No matter how many attempts there are to prevent this from happening, unless interveners themselves can restrain their costs and sense of material entitlement, it is extremely difficult to produce conditions in which those working for the public sector can be retained and rewarded, allowing the state to be strengthened. The significance of this is that we must consider intervention as itself integrally part of, and not separate from, the dynamics of 'development' and accumulation in the spaces in which it unfolds.

Finally, the structural dynamics of what Castel-Branco calls multidimensional aid dependency need to be examined. Although it seems utterly obvious as the foundation of intervention in this context, its political significance as a vector of IR is not always well elaborated – indeed, it is not uncommon for literatures on intervention to ignore it completely. On the one hand, the absolute and relative lack of resources for the host state means that they feel pressure to accept resources from donors, even when accompanied by dubious arrangements, not wholly aligned with what they really want to do, or even obviously potentially damaging. To refuse one source may mean refusing future potential resources, and so in terms of the long game, dependency creates a situation in which the targets of aid have to be much more permissive than they might otherwise be. This means that the seemingly grey zone of political sovereignty – what Harrison and others call the 'sovereign frontier' – is itself fundamentally predicated on dependency – that is, the material need for funds. The flipside of this is that it is much more politically fragile in the longer term than many believe, meaning that the influence of donors also diminishes where other resources become available, either internally or internationally. The rapid diminishing of the power of Western donors once oil and gas revenues were prospected in Mozambique is testament to this fragility.

These structural features that emerge from accounts from below – *protagonismo*, disposability, entitlement and dependency – contribute to widespread and persistent patterns of alienation amongst the targets of intervention, who have now understood very well the gap between what interventions promise and what they deliver. In particular, although 'statebuilding', 'capacity-building' and 'development' are what is intended, the ability to accumulate efforts in any particular direction is heavily limited. It is this which leads to a perception that interventions are not particularly directed at the institutional and human development of the target society, as they profess to be.

COLONIALITY OF POWER AS STRUCTURAL ACCOUNT OF INTERNATIONAL INTERVENTION

Why are these relations so persistent? It is here that the concepts of the 'coloniality of power' and 'colonial difference' help articulate a historical-structural account of global order, in a way which can help us make sense of the persistence of structures of *protagonismo*, disposability, entitlement and dependency within the relationship. Reading from the bottom up, these are not trivial dimensions of the relationship, but *constitutive* features that are resistant to reform and which consistently undo the purported aims of state-building. They should therefore be of significant interest to those who study global relations of power in the present.

The concept of the coloniality of power was developed by Quijano (1992, 2000) to explain the persistence of hierarchical and Western-centric relations in an ostensibly 'postcolonial' world, but has been developed further by others (Mignolo 2002, 2007; Grosfoguel 2002). It ties together the historical emergence of hierarchical concepts of race and culture with the emergence of a capitalist world system centred around Europe, locating both phenomena in the conquest of America. Specifically, it is the argument that 'modernity' in its historic and epistemic co-ordinates cannot be separated from 'coloniality' – that it always carries within it a racist, dualistic hierarchy of the human which enables forms of conquest, appropriation, violence and domination. This has been central to the production of a global division of labour and a nat-uralisation of the entitlements of the West to the products of the non-West – in short, to a global colonial matrix of power. In this sense, formal 'coloni-alism' is itself only one specific historical instantiation of 'coloniality'. As Anghie and others have shown, modern international institutions such as international law and regimes of sovereignty themselves can be read as con-stitutively concerned with the reproduction of colonial and imperial power over the Third World (Anghie 2007; Abrahamsen 2005).

Supposedly 'cosmopolitan' and 'universalist' in its form, modernity is thus produced not through moral and scientific relations of *equivalence* but geocultural relations of colonial difference. Relations of colonial differ-ence attribute primary historical significance and political consciousness to Western subjects and apparently West-centred historical processes, which others are then encouraged to reproduce or into which they are encouraged to integrate themselves. They are partially hegemonic, insofar as they are pro-ductive of a series of identities and ways of being in the world. However, they are also incomplete which means that border spaces of thinking and being-otherwise continue to be produced at the margins of colonial order, replete with potentials for recasting colonial modernity (Anzaldúa 2012 [1999]; Mignolo et al. 2006). Border spaces represent a space for different identities, values, connectivities and ways of thinking and being.

Existing accounts of the coloniality of power and colonial difference tend to operate in a grand historical and rather abstract register, sketching broad connections between accumulations of wealth and the production of know-ledge at a global level. Their contribution is to articulate the situation, often identified with Latin American states and societies, of ongoing structural inequalities and subordination despite a century and a half of political independence and attempted economic development.

The account of international intervention presented in this book, however, shows how this hierarchical, structured bifurcation of Western and non-Western subjects central to modernity (Shilliam 2008) animates the foundational dynamics of intervention in a more detailed, concrete political sense, through the dynamics of *protagonismo*, disposability, entitlement and dependency. Each of these dynamics turns on the political and practical primacy of the interveners and systematically obtains even in a setting in which individuals and institutions try quite hard to avoid or deny racist or colonialist resonances of any kind. Despite this, the organisation of protocols and practices reinscribes colonial difference – that is, a bifurcated humanity – through its framing of who is and who is not important. Thinking about racism in this way, as a feature of the global coloniality of power – a hierarchical division of subjects and entitlements – however, can move the conversation beyond the defensive denials with which discussions of race and racism are often greeted. Rather, we need to think about ways in which the global political order generates, formalises and naturalises forms of political indifference towards non-Western subjects. These structures are arguably prior to debates and issues around 'sovereignty', 'global governance' and 'hybridity', insofar as the latter are questions of world order which in practice presuppose the reality of the coloniality of power.[2] A thought experiment suggested by one of my interlocutors – of a Mozambican going to the United Kingdom to teach its civil servants how to operate – illustrates perfectly the foundational colonial asymmetry that underpins the political dynamics here. Even in a world of blurred boundaries, sovereign frontiers and transnational governance, it remains fundamentally absurd for us to think of multiple African delegations sitting in European countries offering three-year rotating assistance programmes in different sectors, living at much higher standards than the poor communities they intend to help.[3]

When we think about international statebuilding interventions as structured by and through a contemporary global colonial matrix of power – which for many operates as a kind of background common sense even if it is not articulated in the language of coloniality – it becomes relatively obvious why, as a project, it would not work in producing or contributing to the production of autonomous and coherent self-governing political entities. These are conditions where the accumulations of organised authority, resources and expertise in a particular space are challenged by centrifugal dynamics of fragmentation and disposability. This is not to say that individuals in those spaces are not personally powerful or wealthy – indeed, many, including in Mozambique, have carved out spaces for the generation of personal wealth through business opportunities or through servicing the infrastructure of intervention. However, the accumulation of wealth amongst individuals and networks enables the consolidation of regimes who inhabit the state rather than effecting the kinds of cumulative forms of statebuilding and development which they promise.

***

In thinking back to the existing literatures on intervention, this account, rooted in the experiences of its targets and a contemplation of the coloniality of power, helps flesh out a number of lacunae or blind spots within the existing literature. An obvious place to start is with Autesserre's recent award-winning *Peaceland* (2014) – an otherwise empirically excellent account of the everyday dynamics of peacebuilding which broadly correspond to many of those identified here within longer-term statebuilding. Descriptively, Autesserre shows a clear awareness of the primacy of interveners' own wellbeing, protocols and knowledges over what she terms the 'local' and demonstrates multiple ways in which these produce systematic dysfunctionalities and resentments. However, Autesserre's analysis is seriously hamstrung by the inability or refusal to articulate or investigate the colonial and racialised dimensions of this relationship. Rather euphemistically referring to what we would recognise as 'relations of colonial difference' as non-specific 'structures of inequality' between the international and local, she is dismissive of the idea that these could be colonial in form, suggesting that such suggestions are 'conspiracy theories' (204) and citing the presence of African nationals within peacebuilding contingents as evidence that they are not racist. And yet, the characteristic dynamics that she identifies – such as the disregard for 'local knowledge' – are not analysed as being part of any wider political pattern of colonial epistemologies. When we do such analysis, it seems that one reason that 'local knowledge' cannot be seriously incorporated into the logics of intervention is that it can fundamentally challenge the authority of 'thematic experts'. For example, in chapter 6 I demonstrated that 'local knowledge' and understandings of corruption in Mozambique put the ruling elite and the interveners under a moral spotlight which highlighted their hypocrisy, greed and sense of personal entitlement to supposedly public resources. Such forms of consciousness and historical memory could even overturn interveners' implicit claims to epistemic supremacy on matters of anti-corruption.

Even more strangely, Autesserre also analytically disregards accusations of racism and colonial behaviour made by her own respondents, even though they make it into the text. It turns out that the 'listening project', of which ethnography like this should be a key part, is not much of a 'hearing project'. These issues are instead all glossed as problems of practice, which are only institutional problems, and thus de-tethered from any other form of historical knowledge or political relationship. This obtuseness is recurrent but at its most jarring where a respondent has referred to peacebuilders as acting as if they were 'a different species' (2014: 177), calling into explicit and direct focus the bifurcated conception of the human within peacebuilding. For Autesserre, the specificity of this issue is ignored, in favour of more palatable conclusions about the 'daily work routines' of peacebuilders and their social habits, and the need to have 'more positive narratives of local people' (214).

There is much to say here about the reasons why this may be the case, but two points may suffice. The first is that, intellectually, Autesserre's invocation of the 'practice turn' (Bueger et al. 2015) may be incompatible with any form of structural analysis that would explain patterns of practice in terms outside itself. Indeed, she (rightly) calls into question the framing of peacebuilding as 'liberal' given its many non-liberal or un-liberal elements. Yet, this is not a necessary consequence of attention to practice; indeed, insofar as patterns are not idiosyncratic or trivial, they can be understood as structural in character without being deterministic (Wight 2006: chapter 4). The second related point is to do with understandings of both colonialism and racism in Autesserre's epistemological framework. Colonialism is understood to be definitively *historical* (in a past versus present sense) and therefore not part of the present, as is repeatedly made clear – any attempt to suggest a connection is simply dismissed. More interestingly, although Autesserre does – with some courage – address racist attitudes amongst interveners, racism is understood as a function of an individual's own stated misplaced prejudices but not a structural, institutional or collective condition with wider implications. Yet, married with Autesserre's empirical material, the framing of the coloniality of power and relations of colonial difference are analytically powerful – they demonstrate the non-accidental, political and structural character of the problems she identifies, and which are identified in the findings of this book.

At the other end of the spectrum are writers whose conceptual attention to the structural production of intervention frame it as an explicitly ideologically driven political project – of global neoliberal governance and biopolitical containment of 'uninsured' populations (Duffield 2007), of 'riot control' (Duffield 2001; Pugh 2005), of regimes of 'multi-level governance' in the context of the internationalisation of the state (Hameiri 2010) or a hollowed-out 'post-liberalism' (Chandler 2010). These accounts are structural in their orientation, locating international interventions and the 'development-security merger' in terms of a set of wider (neo)liberal global capitalist formations. Where they present detailed engagements with post-conflict or post-crisis environments (and not all do), they also present useful analyses of the ways in which intervention has sought to reform target societies in ways to make them amenable to markets, privatisation, structural adjustment policies and so on. All of these emphasise the changing nature of sovereignty and autonomy under conditions of globalisation and most make the argument that the last few decades were fundamentally about re-engineering states and populations to make them amenable to capital. As argued in chapter 2,

Duffield in particular highlights the need to see contemporary interventions as a continuation of strategies of colonial rule, designed to govern the 'surplus populations' produced by capitalist realignment after the 1970s.

Whilst these accounts are valuable in drawing out what interveners may or may not intend, what the analysis of this book suggests is also a fundamental *indifference* as to whether they succeed or fail in these efforts to govern. In this sense, the analysis resonates with Heathershaw's (2009) account of the performative character of intervention in Tajikistan and, to a smaller extent, Mosse's (2005) account of the politically necessary gap between 'good policy' and functioning practices. Certainly, the present array of policies and outcomes in Mozambique put forward over the last thirty years has not produced a coherently structured, obediently governed space, even from the point of view of liberal and capitalist penetration. Thinking from below, does this really look in any way like a governing project – even a failed one? And if not, what does this tell us? An explanation rooted in questions of the coloniality of power rather than biopolitical governance pushes more towards a constitutive rather than a purposive account of how and why intervention functions the way it does, specifically looking at the roots and features of the hierarchies in place.

Relations of colonial difference are clearly both 'material' and 'epistemic' in character and practice, and they robustly reproduce themselves despite a series of attempted challenges. However, the relation of the 'surplus populations' identified in Duffield's account to the specific contemporary configuration of capital is, on my reading, secondary in an analytic sense to the wider relations of disposability in which they are embedded. In a historical sense – perhaps even epistemically and materially – relations of colonial difference are prior to any specific project of neoliberal governance, and may indeed outlast it. Whilst there is, then, an affinity between this explanation rooted in the coloniality of power and those rooted in the expanded frontier of liberal governance, there are clearly also fruitful questions to debate and which demand further research.

Finally, it is worth saying something about a third literature which suggests that the politics of intervention is characterised by compatibility problems between interveners with their programmes of liberal engineering and 'locals' of various kinds. Although the writers do not use the term, the question of compatibility between interveners and intervened-in societies substantively underpins writings on the 'hybrid peace' (Mac Ginty 2010), the 'post-liberal' peace (Richmond 2012), the 'local turn' (Mac Ginty et al. 2013) and the 'friction' literature (Björkdahl et al. 2013). Perhaps unsurprisingly given the authors' roots in the conflict management and peacebuilding traditions, the emphasis is on societal groupings, values and forms of contestation, rather than between the interveners and the state as a political actor. Thus a wide range of local actors, of whom some are state-based, by turns adapt, resist, are co-opted or coerced by intervention towards the goals of the liberal peace, although it is sometimes recognised that the relationship is asymmetric. This produces various forms of 'hybrid peace' in which the 'liberal' and 'local' are brought together, in either 'negative' or 'positive' forms.

In terms of the findings of this study, the fundamental problems of intervention – and indeed the causes of the alienation and dispossession produced amongst its targets – are *not* 'compatibility' problems caused by a lack of familiarity, cultural fit, understanding or empathy, or tensions between 'liberal' and 'local' ways of doing things, but 'coloniality' problems caused by the well-understood underlying political dynamics of intervention and its bifurcated understanding of who matters.[4] Whilst the 'compatibility' literature acknowledges these issues, and sometimes attempts to run different accounts and explanations together[5] as if they were the same, it does not clarify the political parameters of this problem. Rather, by characterising the actors as 'liberal' and 'local', respectively, the compatibility explanation tends to ontologically depoliticise and de-historicise relations of colonial difference as being about a 'clash of values'.

In sum, whilst there are many accounts of international peacebuilding and statebuilding interventions in circulation, few have attempted to mobilise the ideas of the targets of intervention in building up an analytic framework for explaining the phenomena. Autesserre's approach has been welcomed for its detailed ethnography, but she translates her very striking findings into an oddly blunted, analytically flat set of conclusions. Duffield's comprehensive account is also rich and convincing, but does not embrace the potential of a standpoint form of critique as a means of reinterpreting the political dynamics of intervention. The coloniality of power framework developed here, however, brings together the lived experiences of intervention with a way of making sense of it as a structural, productive dimension of global power. As such, this project also makes a contribution to debates on the coloniality of power by the elaboration of some of its historiographical, epistemological and methodological concerns through an extended illustrative case study in a space of global public policymaking.

(HOW) CAN WE DECOLONISE INTERVENTION?

Given the constitutive, structural account of the coloniality of power which shapes the terrain of intervention, what hope is there that such a relationship can be decolonised? Are there forms of political ethics which can usefully challenge the present dynamics? Is it possible for international intervention to function, such that it does, in a less damaging way? What would this look like? In this concluding discussion, I suggest that, to decolonise intervention, it is necessary to contemplate abandoning its central intellectual assumptions, its modes of operation and its political structures, in order to remake a terrain for solidaristic engagement and, where appropriate, postcolonial reparation. Given the scale of such a transformational demand, short of this, there are also smaller gestures that could nonetheless make a small impact on the conduct of intervention and its political effects.

To recap, the dynamics of intervention identified in this study – *protagonismo*, disposability, entitlement and dependency – all have their roots in what we have called the 'coloniality of power'. This coloniality of power produces a kind of 'common sense' about the modern world, in which the West emerges as an either fortunate or deserving historical genius, which rationalises and justifies its subordination of the rest of the world in political and economic terms. Racialised identities, theories of human development, sciences of anthropology, sociology and economics, concepts of sovereignty and nationhood and so on all cohere to produce a world in which the primacy of the West as a beacon for humanity is taken as given and a benchmark for others to which to aspire.

Yet, a short excursion into the historical rise of the West reveals its embeddedness within global dynamics of interdependence and competition, as well as the history of dirt and blood involved in the growth of capitalism and the rise of the West (Anievas and Nişancıoğlu 2015). Moreover, the emergence of the West as an economic and political entity was itself constitutively bound up with its own imperial integration with the global South; an emblematic example of this is the role of India in furnishing much of the raw materials, labour and technology that drove the Industrial Revolution in Britain (Bhambra 2007). A look at the economic policies and strategies it has recently promoted, however, demonstrates that they are not those which led to its rise – instead, they are much the opposite (Chang 2002).

To recall these histories is to challenge the common sense through which people of the global South are rendered dependent and disposable, whereas their Northern partners are the protagonists of and participants in the machine of human progress. This alternative historiography demonstrates that modern, ostensibly 'Western' phenomena such as 'development' and 'statebuilding' turned on the fundamental interconnectedness of different populations around the world, of which the accumulated wealth of the collective efforts were restricted to particular spaces and peoples due to the racialised sense of entitlement underpinning the wider enterprise. To reject the contemporary reproduction of the racialised character of that entitlement is to make a case for a redistributive postcolonial ethical order, which recognises forms of collective historic responsibility for the nature of this order. Therefore, to reframe North-South international intervention through a decolonising sensibility means, first and foremost, that aid needs to be conceived not as a form of philanthropic assistance from the rich to the poor but a political system of historically engaged reparations working on healing what Mignolo and others have called 'the colonial wound' (2009: 3).

Such a rethinking might lead for a reversed understanding of who deserves what out of intervention – in this story, it is the target of aid who is entitled to it materially by virtue of historical patterns of imperial dispossession. They are also, under this logic, entitled to create the political space for their own sense of *protagonismo* over how to generate collective well-being. As Castel-Branco (2007) argues in his critical account of ownership discourse, it is not enough to simply talk about 'ownership' or 'sovereignty' but to cultivate the material conditions under which chronic aid dependency can be overturned. As noted in the earlier chapters, where Mozambique has been able to generate some freedom of manoeuvre, it has done so, albeit at considerable political cost sometimes, and not always to the benefit of the public.

Interveners, however, need to embrace their diminishing importance and lost moral authority on many aspects of intervention, whilst being ready to assist financially where they are able. This is an unpalatable prospect for those accustomed to a playing field in which they are understood to be naturally entitled to offer expertise, guidance and to exercise control. Specifically, they can look to de-escalate the tendencies for *protagonismo*, disposability, entitlement and dependency within Western intervention, which should reduce some of the immediately harmful impact that aid may have, even as a wider structural transformation is ultimately necessary. Three specific forms of attention to existing practice can be illustrated here briefly.

First, interveners could find ways of accounting for the opportunity costs of their own activities to the targets of intervention. The politics of disposability within intervention is particularly engendered by bureaucratic accounting mechanisms which follow dollars around but do not generally conceive of the intended beneficiaries as expending any resource in order to service the programme. This is, as the study has shown, of course untrue, but it enables interveners to treat beneficiaries as effectively disposable. A more respectful accounting procedure would account for the loss of time and activity occurring as a result of the programme. In the health sector, for example, how many patients would have been attended to, had the worker not been at the programme? How many civil servant hours have been absorbed by this co-operation? In the agricultural sector, what would this land have been used for if not this crop? What was the longer-term effect of this project (i.e. two or three years after the project was finished)? More broadly, have any projects like this been tried before and what was the long-term effect? If the target had the funds, what would they spend them on, and is this more important than what is being suggested? Integrating such considerations and calculations into the planning phase as well as the monitoring and evaluation phases would force a reckoning with the 'real' value of the programme or project on terms set by the intended beneficiary. This would also reframe the conversations around the expensive and ineffective character of many international aid consultancy engagements. Whilst the conservative Western press and political establishment frames these as a waste of taxpayers' money, a decolonising reading of the same sees these costs as principally borne by the intended targets, who not only lose the resources that they might have had to implement a programme but also have to spend time servicing and supporting consultants.

Second, interveners could simply observe the international signed agreements on aid harmonisation and ownership. This is a very basic request on one level, aimed at containing the negative effects of *protagonismo* on the part of donors, but one which Western donors in particular seem fundamentally unable to stomach. Many of the issues with the effects of duplication, ownership and fragmentation were already addressed in the Paris Declaration on Aid Effectiveness (2005) and the Busan Partnership for Effective Development Co-operation (2011) (although neither is an unproblematic document). Yet, the trend for many Western donors in Mozambique has been to withdraw from common funding arrangements and priorities defined by the government, citing a lack of influence and transparency and seeking to develop partnerships outside the state to realise their objectives. This study suggests, however, that, in many respects, the reduction in influence over the development agenda should be viewed as a *positive* outcome politically, if it means that the target government is able to pursue a policy it has defined coherently, supported by resources which are committed to those ends. In the longer term, to have 'traditional donors' seeing themselves more like Southern donors do will mean reckoning with the relations of colonial difference that have historically defined these relationships.

Finally, interveners could think about a deeper politics of postcolonial ethical responsibility regarding global political and economic structures which facilitate dynamics of ongoing dispossession. Whilst certain structural hypocrisies in international development are well known – such as the long-term persistence of EU and US agricultural subsidies, which often disadvantage Southern producers and business, and the roles of the state in subsidising various industries – it has recently become clearer through revelations such as the Panama Papers that Western financial institutions and tax havens are key actors in facilitating elite networks of corruption in the global South (Cooley et al. 2017). These can also be understood as integral to facilitating state collapse (Hill et al. 2013). These situations have to be understood as politically untenable in the light of a stated desire to promote fair and equitable global development, in which power and money are made accountable and accessible to the many rather than the few. Western governments and publics need to refrain from claiming moral authority on these issues and begin with a diagnostic of the multiple sites at which theft and dispossession take place, many of which are within their control.

***

And yet, as this book is being finished, it appears that the global political climate – at least in the West – is moving in another direction. The political consensus of the last few decades offered occasional public glimpses of solidaristic and humanistic sensibilities about world politics, even if deeply embedded in relations of colonial difference, and problematic, hypocritical practices which worked against statebuilding. There were points at which a thin global accountability was promised, even if not delivered. Whilst the old is dying, and the new is not yet born, the morbid, populist-authoritarian-racist-fascist symptoms of the present are not especially promising. It may well be that the ethical imperatives holding together practices of international intervention will simply break and the practices disappear from Western policy in the near future. This may seem unlikely, but, even so, a significant rescaling is almost certainly on the cards.

This presents both an opportunity and a problem for a decolonial political moment. The opportunity may be this: With a West which is less committed to interfering directly in the global South, there is more space for practical 'de-linking', which generates space for autonomous political projects and ways of thinking/being. This may anyway be the consequence of the decline of Western power in its twentieth-century form (Hopgood 2013). The recent rise of leftist governments in South America and elsewhere has partially realised some of these aspirations. However, in looking at the ongoing problems these countries have faced, it is clear that (a) the West is unlikely to seriously disengage from the global South, and (b) politically engaged people in different sites cannot abandon the interconnected character of decolonial politics on issues as diverse as land dispossession, violence against indigenous peoples, offshore tax havens, environmental degradation and the facilitation of war. All of these require a confrontation with the relations of colonial difference that facilitate the globally differentiated entitlements of humans to protection, resources and political space.

With this in mind, the future prospects for the contribution of academic knowledge to a better and more just world will depend on its capacity to work with and through the perspectives of those disempowered by relations of coloniality, across the globe. IR as a discipline is beginning, slowly and surely, to perceive ways in which it might do this. As it develops 'loci of enunciation' beyond its North Atlantic roots, there is the potential for its thinking to become broader, more diverse and more insightful on such issues. In this sense, although the discipline may be late to the party in terms of confronting its colonial thinking, there is plenty more music to come.

NOTES

1. See Giroux (2012), Odysseos (2016).
2. See particularly Anghie (2007: chapter 5).
3. John Heathershaw has drawn my attention to the satire by Megoran (2005).
4. Targets of intervention therefore often develop a fluency in *multiple* political registers, as demonstrated by Heathershaw (2007).
5. See, for example, Richmond (2014: conclusion).

References

Adam, Y. (1990). *Foreign aid to Mozambique: Needs and effects, a preliminary report, Working Paper D 1990:15.* Bergen: Chr. Michelsen Institute.

Agathangelou, A. M. & Ling, L. H. M. (2009). *Transforming world politics: From empire to multiple worlds.* Taylor & Francis.

Alcoff, L. M. (Ed.). (1998). *Epistemology: The big questions.* Malden, MA: Wiley-Blackwell.

Alden, C. (2002). Making old soldiers fade away: Lessons from the reintegration of demobilized soldiers in Mozambique. *Security Dialogue, 33*(3), 341.

Alden, C. & Chichava, S. (Eds.). (2014). *China and Mozambique: From comrades to capitalists.* Jacana Media.

Alfred, T. & Coulthard, G. S. (2014). *Red skin, white masks: Rejecting the colonial politics of recognition.* Minneapolis: University of Minnesota Press.

Anghie, A. (2007). *Imperialism, sovereignty and the making of international law* (Vol. 37). Cambridge University Press.

Anievas, A., Manchanda, N. & Shilliam, R. (2014). *Race and racism in international relations: Confronting the global colour line.* Routledge.

Anievas, A. & Nişancıoğlu, K. (2015). *How the West came to rule: The geopolitical origins of capitalism.* Pluto Press.

Anzaldúa, G. (2012). *Borderlands/La Frontera: The new Mestiza* (4th ed. edition). San Francisco: Aunt Lute Books.

Ascione, G. & Chambers, I. (2016). Global historical sociology: Theoretical and methodological issues – an introduction. *Cultural Sociology, 10*(3), 301–316. https://doi.org/10.1177/1749975516639086.

Autesserre, S. (2010). *The trouble with the Congo: Local violence and the failure of international peacebuilding* (Vol. 115). Cambridge University Press.

Autesserre, S. (2014). *Peaceland: Conflict resolution and the everyday politics of international intervention.* Cambridge University Press.

Azagaia. (2009). Combatentes de Fortuna. *Cotonete Records.* http://www.youtube.com/watch?v=hqkvNKh9Tmw.

Bain, W. (2003). *Between anarchy and society: Trusteeship and the obligations of power.* Oxford: Oxford University Press.

Balibar, E. (1991). Is there a neo-racism? In I. Wallerstein & E. Balibar (Eds.), C. Turner (Trans.), *Race, nation, class: Ambiguous identities.* Verso Books.

Banze, S. (2011, 2 September). Se Samora Machel estivesse vivo, muitos governantes estariam presos. *O País.* Maputo. http://opais.sapo.mz/index.php/politica/ 63-politica/12227-se-samora-machel-estivesse-vivo-muitos-governantes-estariam-presos.html. Accessed 12 January 2012.

Barkawi, T. & Laffey, M. (1999). The imperial peace: Democracy, force and globalization. *European Journal of International Relations, 5*(4), 403–434. https://doi.org/ 10.1177/1354066199005004001.

Barkawi, T. & Laffey, M. (2002). Retrieving the imperial: Empire and international relations. *Millennium: Journal of International Studies, 31*(1), 109–127.

Barkawi, T. & Laffey, M. (2006). The postcolonial moment in security studies. *Review of International Studies, 32*(2), 329–352. https://doi.org/10.1017/ S0260210506007054.

Barnett, M. & Zürcher, C. (2009). The peacebuilder's contract: How external state-building reinforces weak statehood. In R. Paris & T. D. Sisk (Eds.), *The dilemmas of statebuilding: Confronting the contradictions of postwar peace operations* (pp. 23–52). Taylor & Francis.

Batley, R. (2005). Mozambique: The costs of "owning" aid. *Public Administration and Development, 25*(5), 415–424.

Bayart, J. F. & Harper, M. (1993). *The state in Africa: The politics of the belly.* Longman London.

BBC News. (2008). BBC NEWS | Health | Africa "being drained of doctors." Retrieved December 8, 2016, from http://news.bbc.co.uk/1/hi/health/7178978.stm.

BBC News. (2010, September 7). Mozambique reverses bread price rise in wake of riots. *BBC News.* Retrieved from http://www.bbc.co.uk/news/business-11216009.

Begby, E. & Burgess, J. P. (2009). Human security and liberal peace. *Public Reason, 1*(1), 91–104.

Bhambra, G. K. (2007). *Rethinking modernity: Postcolonialism and the sociological imagination.* Palgrave Macmillan.

Bhambra, G. K. (2009). *Rethinking modernity: Postcolonialism and the sociological Imagination.* Palgrave Macmillan.

Bilgin, P. (2008). Thinking past "Western" IR? *Third World Quarterly, 29*(1), 5–23. https://doi.org/10.1080/01436590701726392.

Björkdahl, A. & Höglund, K. (2013). Precarious peacebuilding: Friction in global–local encounters. *Peacebuilding, 1*(3), 289–299. https://doi.org/10.1080/ 21647259.2013.813170.

Blaney, D. L. & Inayatullah, N. (2010). *Savage economics: Wealth, poverty, and the temporal walls of capitalism.* London; New York: Routledge.

Boutros-Ghali, B. (1992). *An agenda for peace: Preventive diplomacy, peacemaking and peace-keeping: Report of the Secretary-General pursuant to the statement adopted by the Summit Meeting of the Security Council on 31 January 1992.* New York: United Nations.

Boutros-Ghali, B. (1995). *An agenda for peace 1995.* New York: United Nations.

Bozzoli, C. & Brück, T. (2009). Agriculture, poverty, and postwar reconstruction: Micro-level evidence from Northern Mozambique. *Journal of Peace Research, 46*(3), 377–397.

Buck-Morss, S. (2009). *Hegel, Haiti, and universal history* (1ST edition). Pittsburgh, PA: University of Pittsburgh Press.

Bueger, C. & Gadinger, F. (2015). The play of international practice. *International Studies Quarterly, 59*(3), 449–460. https://doi.org/10.1111/isqu.12202.

Butler, J. (1990). *Gender trouble: Feminism and the subversion of identity* (1st edition). Routledge.

Cabral, A. (1966). The weapon of theory. *Speech to the Tri-Continental Conference, Havana, Cuba.*

Cabral, A. (1979). *Unity and struggle: Speeches and writings.* Monthly Review Press.

Cabrita, J. M. (2000). *Mozambique: The tortuous road to democracy.* Basingstoke: Palgrave.

Cahen, M. (1987). *Mozambique, la révolution implosée: études sur 12 ans d'indépendance (1975–1987).* Paris: L'Harmattan.

Caldeira, A. (2016, 30 August). "Nunca houve uma política agrária moçambicana," João Mosca. *Verdade.* http://www.verdade.co.mz/tema-de-fundo/35-the-madefundo/59254-nunca-houve-uma-politica-agraria-mocambicana-joao-mosca. Accessed 11 October 2016

Call, C., Wyeth, V. & International Peace Academy. (2008). *Building states to build peace.* Boulder, CO: Lynne Rienner.

Campbell, S., Chandler, D. & Sabaratnam, M. (2011). *A liberal peace? The problems and practices of peacebuilding.* London: Zed Books.

CanalMoz. (2009, 21 May). Editorial: Soberania nacional, legislação e necessidade de medicos, aconselham mais diálogo.

Caplan, R. (2005). *International governance of war-torn territories: Rule and reconstruction.* New York: Oxford University Press.

Carayannis, T. (2016). Peaceland: Conflict resolution and the everyday politics of international intervention. *Cambridge Review of International Affairs, 29*(1), 337–341. https://doi.org/10.1080/09557571.2015.1106067.

Castel-Branco, C. N. (2008). Aid dependency and development: A question of ownership? A critical view. *Maputo: IESE (Working Paper 01/2008).*

Césaire, A. (2000). *Discourse on colonialism.* (R. D. G. Kelley, Ed.). New York: Monthly Review Press.

Césaire, A. (2010). Letter to Maurice Thorez. *Social Text, 28*(2 103), 145.

Chabal, P. (1983). *Amilcar Cabral: Revolutionary leadership and people's war.* Cambridge: Cambridge University Press.

Chakrabarty, D. (2000). *Provincializing Europe: Postcolonial thought and historical difference.* Princeton, NJ: Princeton University Press.

Chambers, R. (1997). *Whose reality counts? Putting the first last* (2nd edition). London: ITDG.

Chandler, D. (1999). *Bosnia: Faking democracy after Dayton.* London; Sterling, VA: Pluto Press.

Chandler, D. (2006). *Empire in denial: The politics of state-building.* London; Ann Arbor, MI: Pluto Press.

Chandler, D. (2009). Critiquing liberal cosmopolitanism? The limits of the biopolitical approach. *International Political Sociology, 3*(1), 53–70.

Chandler, D. (2010a). *International statebuilding: The rise of post-liberal governance.* London; New York: Routledge.

Chandler, D. (2010b). The uncritical critique of "liberal peace." *Review of International Studies, 36*(Supplement S1), 137–155. https://doi.org/10.1017/S0260210510000823.

Chang, H.-J. (2002). *Kicking away the ladder: Development strategy in historical perspective: Policies and institutions for economic development in historical perspective* (1st edition). London: Anthem Press.

Chesterman, S. (2004). *You, the people: The United Nations, transitional administration, and state-building.* Oxford; New York: Oxford University Press.

Chesterman, S. (2008). The sovereignty paradox: The norms and politics of international statebuilding. *American Journal of International Law, 102*(2), 405. https://doi.org/10.2307/30034567.

Chesterman, S., Ignatieff, M. Thakur, R. C., International Peace Academy & United Nations University. (2005). *Making states work: State failure and the crisis of governance.* Tokyo; New York: United Nations University Press.

Coelho, J. P. B. (1998). State resettlement policies in post-colonial rural Mozambique: The impact of the Communal Village Programme on Tete Province, 1977–1982. *Journal of Southern African Studies, 24*(1), 61–91.

Collins, P. H. (1986). Learning from the outsider within: The sociological significance of black feminist thought. *Social Problems, 33*(6), S14–S32. https://doi.org/10.2307/800672.

Collins, P. H. (1997). Comment on Hekman's "Truth and method: Feminist standpoint theory revisited": Where's the power? *Signs, 22*(2), 375–381.

Cooley, A. A. & Heathershaw, J. (2017). *Dictators without borders: Power and money in Central Asia.* New Haven, CT: Yale University Press.

Cox, R. W. (1981). Social forces, states and world orders: Beyond international relations theory. *Millennium: Journal of International Studies, 10*(2), 126–155.

Cramer, C. & Pontara, N. (1998). Rural poverty and poverty alleviation in Mozambique: What's missing from the debate? *The Journal of Modern African Studies, 36*(1), 101–138.

Crocker, C. A., Hampson, F. O. & Aall, P. R. (Eds.). (1996). *Managing global chaos: Sources of and responses to international conflict.* US Institute of Peace Press.

Cunguara, B. & Hanlon, J. (2010, June). Poverty is not being reduced in Mozambique. LSE Crisis States Research Centre. Retrieved from http://www.crisisstates.com/Publications/wp/WP74.2.htm.

Cunguara, B. & Hanlon, J. (2012). Whose wealth is it anyway? Mozambique's outstanding economic growth with worsening rural poverty. *Development and Change, 43*(3), 623–647. https://doi.org/10.1111/j.1467-7660.2012.01779.x.

Cunguara, B. & Kelly, B. (2009). The impact of the PARPA II in promoting the agricultural sector in rural Mozambique. *Maputo.* http://www.Open.Ac.uk/technology/mozambique/p7_1.Shtml. Accessed 15 March 2010.

Cunliffe, P. (2012). Still the spectre at the feast: Comparisons between peacekeeping and imperialism in peacekeeping studies today. *International Peacekeeping, 19*(4), 426–442. https://doi.org/10.1080/13533312.2012.709751.

Darby, P. & Paolini, A. J. (1994). Bridging international relations and postcolonialism. *Alternatives: Global, Local, Political, 19*(3), 371–397.

Da Silva, A. (2015, 23 October). Fenomeno "chupa-sangue" aterroriza cidadãos em Nampula.

De Bragança, A. & Wallerstein, I. M. (1982). *The African liberation reader. Vol. 1, The anatomy of colonialism.* London: Zed Press.

De Renzio, P. & Goldsbrough, D. (2007). IMF programs and health spending: Case study of Mozambique. *Background Paper Prepared by the Working Group on IMF Programs and Health Expenditures, Centre for Global Development, Washington, DC.*

De Renzio, P. & Hanlon, J. (2009). Mozambique: Contested sovereignty? The dilemmas of aid dependence. In L. Whitfield (Ed.), *The politics of aid: African strategies for dealing with donors* (pp. 246–270). Oxford: Oxford University Press. Retrieved from http://ukcatalogue.oup.com/product/9780199560172.do.

De Vletter, F. (2006). Microfinance in Mozambique: Achievements, prospects and challenges. *Mozambique Microfinance Facility.*

Dillon, M. & Reid, J. (2000). Global governance, liberal peace, and complex emergency. *Alternatives: Global, Local, Political, 25*(1), 117–143.

Divjak, B. & Pugh, M. (2008). The political economy of corruption in Bosnia and Herzegovina. *International Peacekeeping, 15*(3), 373–386.

Dobbins, J. (2007). *The beginner's guide to nation-building* (Vol. 557). RAND.

Donovan, C., Zavale, H. & Tschirley, D. L. (2010). *The evaluation of the impacts of title II monetization programs for wheat and crude edible oils in Mozambique, 1997–2007.* Michigan State University, Department of Agricultural, Food, and Resource Economics.

Doornbos, M. (2001). "Good governance": The rise and decline of a policy metaphor? *Journal of Development Studies, 37*(6), 93–108. https://doi.org/10.1080/713601084.

Doty, R. L. (1993). The bounds of "race" in international relations. *Millennium: Journal of International Studies, 22*(3), 443–461. https://doi.org/10.1177/03058298930220031001.

Du Bois, W. E. B. (1994). *The souls of black folk* (New edition). New York: Dover.

Du Bois, W. E. B., Mamdani, M. & Horne, G. (2014). *The world and Africa and color and democracy.* (H. L. G. Jr, Ed.). Oxford University Press USA.

Duffield, M. (2005). Getting savages to fight barbarians: Development, security and the colonial present. *Conflict, Security & Development, 5*(2), 141–159.

Duffield, M. R. (2001). *Global governance and the new wars: The merging of development and security.* London; New York: Zed Books.

Duffield, M. R. (2007). *Development, security and unending war: Governing the world of peoples.* Polity.

Dunford, R. (2015). Peasant activism and the rise of food sovereignty: Decolonising and democratising norm diffusion? *European Journal of International Relations,* 1354066115614382. https://doi.org/10.1177/1354066115614382.

Egerö, B. (1987). *Mozambique: A dream undone: The political economy of democracy, 1975–84.* Uppsala: Nordiska Afrikainstitutet.

Eurosis. (2010). *RELATÓRIO FINAL: AUDITORIA DE DESEMPENHO AO SECTOR AGRÁRIO.* Maputo: Ministry of Finance.

Evans, A., Cabral, L., Wiggins, S., Greeley, M. & Kaur, N. (2007). Formulating and implementing sector-wide approaches in agriculture and rural development: A synthesis report. *Global Donor Platform for Rural Development.* http://www.odi.org. uk/plag/resources/reports/07_SWAP_synthesis_report.pdf.

Fanon, F. (1965). *The wretched of the earth.* London: Penguin.

Fanon, F. (1994). *Toward the African Revolution* (New Evergreen edition). New York: Grove Press / Atlantic Monthly Press.

Fanon, F. (2008). *Black skin, white masks.* London: Pluto.

Ferguson, J. (1990). *The anti-politics machine: Development, depoliticization, and bureaucratic power in Lesotho.* Cambridge: Cambridge University Press.

Ferrinho, P., Sidat, M., Fresta, M. J., Rodrigues, A., Fronteira, I., da Silva, F., Mercer, H., Cabral, J. & Dussault, G. (2009). The training and professional expectations of medical students in Angola, Guinea-Bissau and Mozambique. In *Regional Health Workforce Conference: Human Resources for Health Results (HR) 2*, May 10–14, 2009. Addis Ababa, Ethiopia.

Fox, L., Bardasi, E. & Van den Broeck, K. (2005). *Poverty in Mozambique: Unraveling changes and determinants.* Washington, DC: World Bank.

Frelimo. Comité Central. (1983). *Relatório do Comité Central ao IV Congresso.* Maputo: Partido Frelimo.

Frelimo. Comité Central. (1989). *Relatório do Comité Central ao V Congresso.* Maputo: Partido Frelimo.

Frelimo. Comité Central & Machel, S. (1977). *O Partido e as classes trabalhadoras moçambicanas na edificaçaõ da democracia popular: relatório do Comité Central ao 3. Congresso.* Maputo: Departamento do Trabalho Ideológico da Frelimo.

Fukuyama, F. (1989). The end of history? *The National Interest* (16), 3–18.

Fukuyama, F. (2004). *State-building: Governance and world order in the 21st century.* Ithaca, NY: Cornell University Press.

G20. (2005). *Annual Poverty Report 2005.* Available on the Programme Aid Partners' website: www.pap.org.mz/downloads/rap05.pdf. Accessed 22 August 2011.

Geffray, C. (1990). *La cause des armes au Mozambique: anthropologie d'une guerre civile.* Paris: Karthala.

Gengenbach, H. (2005). *Binding memories: Women as makers and tellers of history in Magude, Mozambique.* Columbia University Press.

Ghani, A. & Lockhart, C. (2009). *Fixing failed states: A framework for rebuilding a fractured world.* New York: Oxford University Press.

Gilroy, P. (1993). *The black Atlantic: Modernity and double consciousness.* Harvard University Press.

Giroux, H. A. (2012). *Disposable youth: Racialized memories, and the culture of cruelty.* Routledge.

Go, J. (2016). *Postcolonial thought and social theory.* New York, NY: Oxford University Press USA.

Gong, G. W. (1984). *The standard of "civilization" in international society.* Oxford: Clarendon.

Goodhand, J. (2005). Frontiers & wars: The opium economy in Afghanistan. *Journal of Agrarian Change, 5*(2), 191–216.

Gordon, L. R. (1995). *Fanon and the crisis of European man: An essay on philosophy and the human sciences.* New York: Routledge.

Government of Mozambique. (2007). *Final evaluation of the first phase of the National Agricultural Programme PROAGRI (1999–2005) Volume I: Main Report.*

Government of Mozambique. (2010). Moçambique: Avaliação da Declaração de Paris. Ministry of Planning and Development.

Gray, R. (1982). "Khalai-Khalai": People's history in Mozambique. *History Workshop, 14*, 143.

Grindle, M. S. & Hilderbrand, M. E. (1995). Building sustainable capacity in the public sector: What can be done? *Public Administration and Development, 15*(5), 441–463. https://doi.org/10.1002/pad.4230150502.

Grosfoguel, R. (2002). Colonial difference, geopolitics of knowledge, and global coloniality in the modern/colonial capitalist world-system. *Review (Fernand Braudel Center), 25*(3), 203–224.

Grovogui, S. N. (1996). *Sovereigns, quasi sovereigns and Africans: Race and self-determination in international law* (Minnesota Archi edition). Minneapolis: University of Minnesota Press.

Gruffydd Jones, B. (2006). *Decolonizing international relations.* Lanham, MD: Rowman & Littlefield.

Hall, M. & Young, T. (1997). *Confronting leviathan: Mozambique since independence.* London: Hurst.

Hameiri, S. (2010). *Regulating statehood: State building and the transformation of the global order* (2010 edition). Basingstoke; New York: Palgrave Macmillan.

Hameiri, S. (2014). The crisis of liberal peacebuilding and the future of statebuilding. *International Politics, 51*(3), 316–333. https://doi.org/10.1057/ip.2014.15.

Hameiri, S. & Jones, L. (2015). Global governance as state transformation. *Political Studies.* https://doi.org/10.1111/1467–9248.12225.

Hanlon, J. (1984). *Mozambique: The revolution under fire.* London: Zed Books.

Hanlon, J. (1996). *Peace without profit: How the IMF blocks rebuilding in Mozambique.* Oxford: James Currey.

Hanlon, J. (2003). *Siba-Siba Macuacua's killer arrested among growing anti-corruption climate.* Southern African Documentation and Co-operation Centre.

Hanlon, J. (2004). Do donors promote corruption? The case of Mozambique. *Third World Quarterly, 25*(4), 747–763.

Hanlon, J. & Smart, T. (2008). *Do bicycles equal development in Mozambique?* Oxford: James Currey.

Haraway, D. (1988). Situated knowledges: The science question in feminism and the privilege of partial perspective. *Feminist Studies, 14*(3), 575–599. https://doi.org/10.2307/3178066.

Harding, S. (1991). *Whose science? Whose knowledge? Thinking from women's lives* (1st edition). Ithaca, NY: Cornell University Press.

Harding, S. (1998). *Is science multicultural? Postcolonialisms, feminisms, and epistemologies* (1st edition). Bloomington: Indiana University Press.

Harding, S. G. (2004). Rethinking standpoint epistemology: What is "strong objectivity"? In S. G. Harding (Ed.), *The feminist standpoint theory reader: Intellectual and political controversies.* Psychology Press.

Harding, S. G. & Hintikka, M. (1983). *Discovering reality: Feminist perspectives on epistemology, metaphysics, methodology, and philosophy of science.* Kluwer Academic.

Harrison, G. (1999). Corruption as boundary politics: The state, democratisation, and Mozambique's unstable liberalisation. *Third World Quarterly, 20*(3), 537–550.

Harrison, G. (2000). *The politics of democratisation in rural Mozambique : Grassroots governance in Mecúfi.* Lewiston, NY: Edwin Mellen.

Harrison, G. (2004). *The World Bank and Africa: The construction of governance states* (1st edition). London: Routledge.

Hartsock, N. C. M. (2004). The feminist standpoint: Developing the ground for a specifically feminist historical materialism. In S. G. Harding (Ed.), *The feminist standpoint theory reader: Intellectual and political controversies.* Psychology Press.

Haslam, J. (2000). *The vices of integrity: E.H. Carr, 1892–1982* (New edition). London; New York: Verso Books.

Heathershaw, J. (2007). Peacebuilding as practice: Discourses from post-conflict Tajikistan. *International Peacekeeping, 14*(2), 219–236.

Heathershaw, J. (2008). Unpacking the liberal peace: The dividing and merging of peacebuilding discourses. *Millennium: Journal of International Studies, 36*(3), 597–621. https://doi.org/10.1177/03058298080360031101.

Heathershaw, J. (2009). *Post-conflict Tajikistan: The politics of peacebuilding and the emergence of legitimate order.* Routledge.

Hekman, S. (1997). Truth and method: Feminist standpoint theory revisited. *Signs, 22*(2), 341–365.

Helman, G. B. & Ratner, S. R. (1992). Saving failed states. *Foreign Policy* (89), 3–20. https://doi.org/10.2307/1149070.

Henriksen, T. H. (1978). *Mozambique: A history.* London.

Hill, G., Salisbury, P., Northedge, L. & Kinninmont, J. (2013). Yemen: Corruption, capital flight and global drivers of conflict. *Chatham House Report* (September), Chatham House, London. https://www.chathamhouse.org/publications/papers/view/194239#Sthash.cy6mP0Sn.dpuf.

Hill, J. (2005). Beyond the Other? A postcolonial critique of the failed state thesis. *African Identities, 3*(2), 139–154. https://doi.org/10.1080/14725840500235381.

Hindess, B. (2007). The past is another culture. *International Political Sociology, 1*(4), 325–338. https://doi.org/10.1111/j.1749-5687.2007.00024.x.

Hobson, J. M. (2004). *The Eastern origins of Western civilization.* Cambridge: Cambridge University Press.

Hobson, J. M. (2007). Is critical theory always for the white West and for Western imperialism? Beyond Westphilian towards a post-racist critical IR. *Review of International Studies, 33*(S1), 91–116.

Hobson, J. M. (2012). *The Eurocentric conception of world politics: Western international theory, 1760–2010.* Cambridge: Cambridge University Press.

Honwana, R. & Isaacman, A. F. (1988). *The life history of Raúl Honwana: An inside view of Mozambique from colonialism to independence, 1905–1975.* Boulder; London: Rienner.

Hopgood, S. (2013). *The endtimes of human rights.* Cornell University Press.

Hutchings, K. (2003). *Hegel and feminist philosophy.* Oxford: Polity Press. Retrieved from http://www.polity.co.uk/book.asp?ref=9780745619514.

Hutchings, K. (2008). *Time and world politics: Thinking the present.* Manchester; New York: Manchester University Press.

IMF. (2007). *Republic of Mozambique: Poverty Reduction Strategy Paper* (IMF Country Report No. 07/37). Washington, D.C.

Inayatullah, N. & Blaney, D. L. (2003). *International relations and the problem of difference.* New York; London: Routledge.

Iñiguez de Heredia, M. (2017). *Everyday resistance, peacebuilding and state-making: Insights from "Africa's World War."* (E.-P. Guittet, Ed.). Manchester University Press.

Iñiguez de Heredia, M. (2012). Escaping statebuilding: Resistance and civil society in the Democratic Republic of Congo. *Journal of Intervention and Statebuilding, 6*(1), 75–89. https://doi.org/10.1080/17502977.2012.655567.

Instituto Nacional de Estatística. (1999). *Relatório Final do Inquérito aos Agregados Familiar Sobre Orçamento Familiar, 1997–98.* Maputo: Instituto Nacional de Estatística.

Instituto Nacional de Estatística. (2004). *Relatório Final do Inquérito aos Agregados Familiar Sobre Orçamento Familiar, 2002–03.* Maputo: Instituto Nacional de Estatística.

International Civil Service Commission. (2011). Mozambique. http://icsc.un.org/resources/getdata.asp?rpt=pac&id=Mozambique. Accessed 8 September 2011.

Isaacman, A. F. (1995). *Cotton is the mother of poverty: Peasants, work and rural struggle in colonial Mozambique, 1938–61.* Portsmouth, NH: Heinemann; London: James Currey.

Isaacman, A. F. & Isaacman, B. (1976). *The tradition of resistance in Mozambique: The Zambesi Valley, 1850–1921.* University of California Press.

Isaacman, A., Stephen, M., Adam, Y., Homen, M. J., Macamo, E. & Pililao, A. (1980). "Cotton is the mother of poverty": Peasant resistance to forced cotton production in Mozambique, 1938–1961. *The International Journal of African Historical Studies, 13*(4), 581–615. https://doi.org/10.2307/218197.

Jabri, V. (2007). Michel Foucault's analytics of war: The social, the international, and the racial. *International Political Sociology, 1*(1), 67–81. https://doi.org/10.1111/j.1749-5687.2007.00005.x.

Jone, C. (2005). *Press and democratic transition in Mozambique, 1990–2000.* Johannesburg: IFAS Research.

Jones, L. (2011). Reviews: Critical interventions on statebuilding. *Journal of Intervention and Statebuilding, 5*(2), 235–260.

Joseph, J. (2010). The limits of governmentality: Social theory and the international. *European Journal of International Relations, 16*(2), 223.

Krishna, S. (1993). The importance of being ironic: A postcolonial view on critical international relations theory. *Alternatives: Global, Local, Political, 18*, 385–385.

Kumar, K. (1997). *Rebuilding societies after civil war: Critical roles for international assistance.* Boulder, CO: L. Rienner.

Laffey, M. & Nadarajah, S. (2012). The hybridity of liberal peace: States, diasporas and insecurity. *Security Dialogue, 43*(5), 403–420. https://doi.org/10.1177/0967010612457974.

Laffey, M. & Weldes, J. (2008). Decolonizing the Cuban Missile Crisis. *International Studies Quarterly, 52*(3), 555–577.

Lederach, J. P. (1997). *Building peace: Sustainable reconciliation in divided societies.* Washington, DC: United States Institute of Peace Press.

Lemay-Hébert, N. (2009). Statebuilding without nation-building? Legitimacy, state failure and the limits of the institutionalist approach. *Journal of Intervention and Statebuilding, 3*(1), 21–45. https://doi.org/10.1080/17502970802608159.

Lemay-Hébert, N. (2011). The bifurcation of the two worlds: Assessing the gap between internationals and locals in state-building processes. *Third World Quarterly, 32*(10), 1823–1841. https://doi.org/10.1080/01436597.2011.610578.

Long, D. & Schmidt, B. C. (2005). *Imperialism and internationalism in the discipline of international relations.* Cambridge University Press.

Mabunda, L. (2010, 23 October). Os tiros de Jorge Rebelo e Graça Machel. *O País.* Maputo.

Macamo, E. S. (2006). Political governance in Mozambique. DfID.

Macauhub. (2010, 19 March). Producers threaten to bring production of jatropha to an end in Mozambique's Nampula province. http://www.macauhub.com.mo/en/2010/03/19/8780. Accessed on 12 December 2016.

Mac Ginty, R. (2011). *International peacebuilding and local resistance: Hybrid forms of peace.* Basingstoke: Palgrave.

Magaia, L. (1988). *Dumba nengue, run for your life: Peasant tales of tragedy in Mozambique; translated by Michael Wolfers; historical introduction by Allen Issaacman.* Trenton, NJ: Africa World Press.

Marshall, J. (1990). Structural adjustment and social policy in Mozambique. *Review of African Political Economy, 17*(47), 28–43. https://doi.org/10.1080/03056249008703846.

Marshall, J. M. (1993). *Literacy, power and democracy in Mozambique: The governance of learning from colonization to the present.* Boulder: Westview Press.

Maússe, I. & Mudumbe, R. (2015, 26 June). The distribution of wealth as basis for reducing corruption. *Notícias*, Maputo.

McCarthy, T. (2009). *Race, empire, and the idea of human development.* Cambridge: Cambridge University Press.

McCulloch, J. (1983). *In the twilight of revolution: The political theory of Amilcar Cabral.* London; Boston: Routledge & Kegan Paul.

McWha, I. (2011). The roles of, and relationships between, expatriates, volunteers, and local development workers. *Development in Practice, 21*(1), 29–40.

Megoran, N. (2005). Preventing conflict by building civil society: Post-development theory and a central Asian–UK policy success story. *Central Asian Survey, 24*(1), 83–96. https://doi.org/10.1080/02634930500050032.

Mignolo, W. (2002). The geopolitics of knowledge and the colonial difference. *The South Atlantic Quarterly, 101*(1), 57–96.

Mignolo, W. D. (2007). DELINKING. *Cultural Studies*, 21(2–3), 449–514. https://doi.org/10.1080/09502380601162647.

Mignolo, W. D. (2009). Epistemic disobedience, independent thought and decolonial freedom. *Theory, Culture & Society, 26*(7–8), 159–181. https://doi.org/10.1177/0263276409349275.

Mignolo, W. D. & Tlostanova, M. V. (2006). Theorizing from the borders shifting to geo- and body-politics of knowledge. *European Journal of Social Theory, 9*(2), 205–221. https://doi.org/10.1177/1368431006063333.

Millar, G. (2014). Disaggregating hybridity. Why hybrid institutions do not produce predictable experiences of peace. *Journal of Peace Research, 51*(4), 501–514. https://doi.org/10.1177/0022343313519465.

Mills, C. (1998). Alternative epistemologies. In L. M. Alcoff (Ed.), *Epistemology: The big questions* (pp. 392–410). Malden, MA: Wiley-Blackwell.

Ministry of Agriculture. (2007). *Trabalho de Inquérito Agrícola 2007.* Maputo: Ministry of Agriculture.

Ministry of Agriculture and Food Security. (n.d.). *Anuário de Estatísticas Agrárias 2012–2014.* Maputo: Ministry of Agriculture and Food Security.

Mitchell, A. (2011). Quality/control: International peace interventions and "the every-day." *Review of International Studies, 37*(4), 1623–1645.

Mohanty, C. T. (1988). Under Western eyes: Feminist scholarship and colonial dis-courses. *Feminist Review*, 61–88.

Mohanty, C. T. (2003). *Feminism without borders: Decolonizing theory, practicing solidarity.* Durham; London: Duke University Press.

Mohanty, S. P. (1993). The epistemic status of cultural identity: On "beloved" and the postcolonial condition. *Cultural Critique* (24), 41–80. https://doi.org/10.2307/1354129.

Moreira, E. (1947). Portuguese colonial policy. *Africa, 17*(3), 181–191.

Mosca, J. (1999). *A Experiência socialista em Moçammbique (1975–1986).* Lisboa: Instituto Piaget.

Mosca, J. (2011). *Políticas Agrárias de (em) Moçambique, 1975–2009.* Maputo: Escolar Editoria.

Mosse, D. (2005). *Cultivating development: An ethnography of aid policy and prac-tice* (4th ed. edition). London; Ann Arbor, MI: Pluto Press.

Mosse, D. (Ed.). (2013). *Adventures in Aidland: The anthropology of professionals in international development.* Oxford: Berghahn Books.

Mosse, M. (2004). Armando Guebuza: The new Frelimo candidate. *African Security Studies, 13*(1), 79–82.

Mosse, M. (2006). *Uma Breve Analise da Estrategia Anti-Corrupção.* Maputo: Centro de Integridade Pùblica.

Mosse, M. (2007). *Carta Aberta a Hu Jintao.* Maputo: Centro de Integridade Pùblica.

Mucavele, A. (2005). "Samora fez contas ao contrário," jornalista Machado da Graça ao "vt." *Vertical*, Maputo.

Munslow, B. (1990). Mozambique: Marxism-Leninism in reverse, the Fifth Congress of Frelimo. *Journal of Communist Studies and Transition Politics, 6*(1), 109–112.

Muppidi, H. (2012). *The colonial signs of international relations.* Columbia University Press.

Negrão, J. & NetNews. (2009). *Mozambique, Portugal, agree to set up $500m invest-ment bank.* South African Regional Poverty Network. http://www.sarpn.org/docu-ments/d0000002/P18_p_PARPA.pdf. Accessed 16 August 2011.

Newitt, M. D. D. (1995). *A history of Mozambique.* London: C. Hurst.

Nhamirre, B. (2011, 28 January). Samora Machel auferia 60 mil escudos em 1975 e sem direitos a abonos adicionais. *CanalMoz*, Maputo.

Nhampossa, D. (2007). *Speech given to the EU Forum on sustainable development.*

Nhantumbo, N. (2007). *Africa, Moçambique Sem Coerêncía não há Boa Governação.* Durban: Just Done Productions.

Nuvunga, A. (2007). Aid dependence and governance in Mozambique. In *Foreign aid, governance and institutional development in Mozambique.* Maastricht: Shaker.

ODI. (2014). Against the odds: Mozambique's gains in primary health care. https://www.odi.org/sites/odi.org.uk/files/odi-assets/publications-opinion-files/9073.pdf.

Odysseos, L. (2016). Human rights, self-formation and resistance in struggles against disposability: Grounding Foucault's "theorizing practice" of counter-conduct in Bhopal. *Global Society, 30*(2), 179–200. https://doi.org/10.1080/13600826.2016.1141178.

O País. (2009, 3 August). Corrupção é mesmo que sugar o sangue de um irmão.

O País. (2011, 11 February). Complexidade dos casos condiciona celeridade processual.

Orre, A. & Forquilha, S. C. (2012). Uma iniciativa condenada ao sucesso. O fundo distrital dos 7 milhões e suas consequências para a governação em Moçambique. In *Moçambique-Descentralizar o Centralismo. Economia Política, Processos, Resultados.* Maputo: Instituto de Estudos Sociais e Económicos.

Otoo, S., Agapitova, N. & Behrens, J. (2009). The capacity development results framework: A strategic and results-oriented approach to learning for capacity development. World Bank Institute.

Paffenholz, T. (2015). Unpacking the local turn in peacebuilding: A critical assessment towards an agenda for future research. *Third World Quarterly, 36*(5), 857–874. https://doi.org/10.1080/01436597.2015.1029908.

Paris, R. (1997). Peacebuilding and the limits of liberal internationalism. *International Security, 22*(2), 54–89.

Paris, R. (2004). *At war's end: Building peace after civil conflict.* Cambridge; New York, NY: Cambridge University Press.

Paris, R. (2010). Saving liberal peacebuilding. *Review of International Studies, 36*(2), 337–365.

Pavignani, E. & Durao, J. (1999). Managing external resources in Mozambique: Building new aid relationships on shifting sands? *Health Policy and Planning, 14*(3), 243.

Pfeiffer, J. (2003). International NGOs and primary health care in Mozambique: The need for a new model of collaboration. *Social Science & Medicine, 56*(4), 725–738.

Pfeiffer, J. & Chapman, R. (2015). An anthropology of aid in Africa. *The Lancet, 385*(9983), 2144–2145. https://doi.org/10.1016/S0140-6736(15)61013-3.

Pham, Q. & Shilliam, R. (Eds.). (2016). *Meanings of Bandung.* London: Rowman & Littlefield.

Pimentel Teixeira, J. (2003). Ma-Tuga no mato: Imagens sobre os portugueses em discursos rurais moçambicanos. *Lusotopie*, 91–112.

Pitcher, M. A. (1996). Recreating colonialism or reconstructing the state? Privatisation and politics in Mozambique. *Journal of Southern African Studies, 22*(1), 49–74.

Pitcher, M. A. (2002). *Transforming Mozambique: The politics of privatization, 1975–2000.* New York: Cambridge University Press.

Pitcher, M. A. (2006). Forgetting from above and memory from below: Strategies of legitimation and struggle in postsocialist Mozambique. *Africa, 76*(1), 88–112.

Pouligny, B. (2006). *Peace operations seen from below: U.N. missions and local people.* London: C. Hurst.

Prakash, G. (1994). Subaltern studies as postcolonial criticism. *The American Historical Review, 99*(5), 1475–1490.

Pugh, M. (2005). The political economy of peacebuilding: A critical theory perspective. *International Journal of Peace Studies, 10*(2), 23.

Pugh, M. (2008). Employment, labour rights and social resistance. In *Whose peace? Critical perspectives on the political economy of peacebuilding.* Basingstoke: Palgrave Macmillan.

Pugh, M. C. (2000). *Regeneration of war-torn societies.* Basingstoke: Macmillan.

Pugh, M., Cooper, N., & Turner, M. (2008). *Whose peace? Critical perspectives on the political economy of peacebuilding.* Basingstoke: Palgrave.

Quijano, A. (1992). Colonialidad y modernidad/racionalidad. *Perú Indígena, 13*(29), 11–20.

Quijano, A. (2000). Coloniality of power and Eurocentrism in Latin America. *International Sociology, 15*(2), 215–232. https://doi.org/10.1177/0268580900015002005.

Rampton, D. & Nadarajah, S. (2016). A long view of liberal peace and its crisis. *European Journal of International Relations.* https://doi.org/10.1177/1354066116649029.

Randazzo, E. (2016). The paradoxes of the "everyday": Scrutinising the local turn in peace building. *Third World Quarterly, 37*(8), 1351–1370. https://doi.org/10.1080/01436597.2015.1120154.

Rao, R. (2010). *Third World protest: Between home and the world.* Oxford University Press.

Ratilal, P. (1990). *Mozambique: Using aid to end emergency.* New York: UNDP.

Reed, A. L. (1997). *W.E.B. Du Bois and American political thought: Fabianism and the color line.* New York: Oxford University Press.

Richmond, O. (2010). Resistance and the post-liberal peace. *Millennium: Journal of International Studies, 38*(3), 665–692.

Richmond, O. (2011). *A post-liberal peace.* Milton Park, Abingdon, Oxon, England; New York: Routledge.

Richmond, O. (2014). *Failed statebuilding: Intervention, the state, and the dynamics of peace formation.* New Haven: Yale University Press.

Richmond, O. P. (2007). *The transformation of peace* (2005 edition). Basingstoke: Palgrave.

Richmond, O. P. & Franks, J. (2009). *Liberal peace transitions: Between statebuilding and peacebuilding.* Edinburgh University Press.

Richmond, O. P. & Mitchell, A. (Eds.). (2011). *Hybrid forms of peace: From everyday agency to post-liberalism* (2012 edition). Houndmills, Basingstoke, Hampshire; New York: AIAA.

Rotberg, R. I. (2003). *When states fail: Causes and consequences.* Princeton: Princeton University Press.

Ruddick, S. (1980). Maternal thinking. *Feminist Studies, 6*(2), 342–367. https://doi.org/10.2307/3177749.

Rutazibwa, O. U. (2014). Studying Agaciro: Moving beyond Wilsonian intervention-ist knowledge production on Rwanda. *Journal of Intervention and Statebuilding,* *8*(4), 291–302. https://doi.org/10.1080/17502977.2014.964454.

Sabaratnam, M. (2011a). IR in dialogue … but can we change the subjects? A typology of decolonising strategies for the study of world politics. *Millennium: Journal of International Studies, 39*(3), 781–803. https://doi.org/10.1177/0305829811404270.

Sabaratnam, M. (2011b). The liberal peace? A brief intellectual history of inter-national conflict management, 1990–2010. In S. Campbell, D. Chandler, & M. Sabaratnam (Eds.), *A liberal peace? The problems and practices of peacebuilding.* London: Zed Books. http://eprints.soas.ac.uk/17065.

Sabaratnam, M. (2013). Avatars of Eurocentrism in the critique of the liberal peace. *Security Dialogue, 44*(3), 259–278. https://doi.org/10.1177/0967010613485870.

Said, E. W. (2003). *Orientalism* (25th Anniversary edition with 1995 afterword). Penguin Books.

Sandoval, C. (2004). U.S. Third World feminism: The theory and method of oppos-itional consciousness. In S. G. Harding (Ed.), *The feminist standpoint theory reader: Intellectual and political controversies* (pp. 195–209). Psychology Press.

Scott, D. (2004). *Conscripts of modernity: The tragedy of colonial enlightenment.* Durham: Duke University Press.

Scott, J. C. & Ebrary Sub. (1998). *Seeing like a state: How certain schemes to improve the human condition have failed.* New Haven: Yale University Press. Retrieved from http://site.ebrary.com/lib/soas/Doc?id=10210235.

Serra, C. (2002). *Colera e catarse: infra-estruturas sociais de um mito nas zonas costeiras de Nampula (1998/2002).* Imprensa Universitâaria, Universidade Eduardo Mondlane.

Serra, C. (2015, 23 October). Chupa-sangue em Nampula. http://oficinadesociologia. blogspot.co.uk/2015/10/chupa-sangue-em-nampula-1.html.

Shilliam, R. (2006). What about Marcus Garvey? Race and the transformation of sov-ereignty debate. *Review of International Studies, 32*(3), 379–400. https://doi.org/ 10.1017/S0260210506007078.

Shilliam, R. (2008). What the Haitian Revolution might tell us about development, security, and the politics of race. *Comparative Studies in Society and History, 50*(3), 778–808. https://doi.org/10.1017/S0010417508000339.

Shilliam, R. (2009). A Fanonian critique of Lebow's *A cultural theory of international relations. Millennium: Journal of International Studies, 38*(1), 117–136.

Shilliam, R. (2010). The perilous but unavoidable terrain of the non-West. In R. Shilliam (Ed.), *International relations and non-Western thought: Imperialism, colonialism and investigations of global modernity* (pp. 12–26). Routledge.

Shilliam, R. (2011). Decolonising the grounds of ethical inquiry: A dialogue between Kant, Foucault and Glissant. *Millennium: Journal of International Studies, 39*(3), 649.

Shilliam, R. (2014). "Open the gates mek we repatriate": Caribbean slavery, con-structivism, and hermeneutic tensions. *International Theory, 6*(2), 349–372. https:// doi.org/10.1017/S1752971914000165.

Shilliam, R. (2015). *The black Pacific* (Paperback edition). Bloomsbury Academic.

Shilliam, R. (2016). On Africa in Oceania: Thinking besides the subaltern. *Theory, Culture & Society, 33*(7–8), 374–381. https://doi.org/10.1177/0263276416676346.

Shilliam, R. (2017). Race and revolution at Bwa Kayiman. *Millennium: Journal of International Studies, 45*(3).

Smart, T. & Hanlon, J. (2014). *Chickens and beer: A recipe for agricultural growth in Mozambique.* Bicycles+Development.

Smirl, L. (2015). *Spaces of aid: How cars, compounds and hotels shape humanitarianism.* Zed Books.

Smith, D. E. (2004 [1974]). Women's perspective as a radical critique of sociology. In S. G. Harding (Ed.), *The feminist standpoint theory reader: Intellectual and political controversies* (pp. 21–33). Psychology Press.

Smith, L. T. (1999). *Decolonizing methodologies: Research and indigenous peoples.* Zed Books.

Stiglitz, J. E. (1998). More instruments and broader goals: Moving toward the post-Washington consensus: WIDER Annual Lecture. *UNU,* Washington, Jan. 7.

Sumich, J., London School of, E., Political, S. & Crisis States Research, C. (2007). *The illegitimacy of democracy? Democratisation and alienation in Maputo, Mozambique.* Crisis States Research Centre.

Tadjbakhsh, S. (2011). *Rethinking the liberal peace: External models and local alternatives.* Taylor & Francis.

Thompson, D. (2014). Through, against and beyond the racial state. In A. Anievas, N. Manchanda, & R. Shilliam (Eds.), *Race and racism in international relations: Confronting the global colour line* (pp. 44–61). Routledge.

Thurlow, J. (2013). *Evaluating Mozambique's agricultural investment plan.* http://fsg.afre.msu.edu/Mozambique/caadp/Thurlow_Evaluating_Mozambique's_Agricultural_Investment_Plan.pdf.

Turner, D. M. & Shweiki, O. (Eds.). (2014). *Decolonizing Palestinian political economy: De-development and beyond* (2014 edition). Houndmills, Basingstoke, Hampshire; New York: Palgrave Macmillan.

Turner, M. & Kühn, F. P. (Eds.). (2015). *The politics of international intervention: The tyranny of peace.* London; New York: Routledge.

Tvedten, I., Paulo, M. & Rosario, C. (2006). *"Opitanha" social relations of rural poverty in northern Mozambique.* Chr. Michelsen Institute.

UNAC, & GRAIN. (2015). *The land grabbers of the Nacala Corridor: A new era of struggle against colonial plantations in Northern Mozambique* (p. 17). Barcelona.

UNDP. (1994). *Human development report 1994.* New York; Oxford: Oxford University Press.

UNDP Mozambique. (2008). *National human development report.* Maputo: UNDP. http://www.undp.org.mz/en/Publications/National-Reports/Mozambique-National-Human-Development-Report-2008.

USAID. (2005). *USAID anticorruption strategy.* Washington, DC.

US State Department. (2011a). Hardship allowances. Retrieved September 7, 2011, from http://aoprals.state.gov/Web920/hardship.asp, http://aoprals.state.gov/Web920/cola.asp.

US State Department. (2011b). Housing allowance. http://aoprals.state.gov/Web920/lqa_all.asp. Accessed 6 September 2011.

US State Department. (2011c). Per diem allowances, Mozambique. http://aoprals.state.gov/web920/per_diem_action.asp?MenuHide=1&CountryCode=1227. Accessed 7 September 2011.

Vail, L. & White, L. (1980). *Capitalism and colonialism in Mozambique: A study of Quelimane District.* London: Heinemann.

Valoi, E. (2013). Mozambique gets millions of dollars of aid money for nothing | Southern Africa. Retrieved December 8, 2016, from http://www.theafricareport. com/Southern-Africa/mozambique-gets-millions-of-dollars-of-aid-money-for-nothing.html.

@Verdade. (2016, 22 January). Editorial: Revoltante! *@Verdade Online.* Retrieved from http://www.verdade.co.mz/opiniao/editorial/56599.

Vitalis, R. (2000). The graceful and generous liberal gesture: Making racism invisible in American international relations. *Millennium: Journal of International Studies, 29*(2), 331–356.

Vitalis, R. (2015). *White world order, black power politics: The birth of American international relations.* Ithaca: Cornell University Press.

Walker, R. B. J. (1993). *Inside/outside: International relations as political theory.* Cambridge University Press.

Wallerstein, I. (1997). Eurocentrism and its avatars: The dilemmas of social science. *New Left Review, 226,* 93–108.

Wei, S.-J. (2001). *Corruption and Globalization.* Brookings Institute. https://www. brookings.edu/research/corruption-and-globalization.

Weinstein, J. M. (2002). Mozambique: A fading UN success story. *Journal of Democracy, 13*(1), 141–156.

West, H. G. (2005). *Kupilikula: Governance and the invisible realm in Mozambique.* Chicago: University of Chicago Press.

West, H. G. (2008a). From socialist chiefs to postsocialist cadres: Neotraditional authority in neoliberal Mozambique. In H. G. West & P. Raman (Eds.), *Enduring socialism: Explorations of revolution and transformation, restoration and continuation* (pp. 29–43). Oxford: Berghahn. http://eprints.soas.ac.uk/7128.

West, H. G. (2008b). "Govern yourselves!": Democracy and carnage in Northern Mozambique. In J. Paley (Ed.), *Democracy: Anthropological approaches* (pp. 97–121). Santa Fe: School of Advanced Research Press. http://eprints.soas.ac.uk/7129.

West, H. G. & Kloeck-Jenson, S. (1999). Betwixt and between: "Traditional authority" and democratic decentralization in post-war Mozambique. *African Affairs, 98*(393), 455–484.

WHO. (2015). Maternal mortality 1990–2015.

Wilder, G. (2015). *Freedom time: Negritude, decolonization, and the future of the world.* Durham; London: Duke University Press.

Williams, D. (2008). *The World Bank and social transformation in international politics: Liberalism, governance and sovereignty.* London: Routledge.

Williams, D. (2013). Development, intervention, and international order. *Review of International Studies, 39*(05), 1213–1231. https://doi.org/10.1017/S0260210513000260.

Williams, D. & Young, T. (1994). Governance, the World Bank and liberal theory. *Political Studies, 42*(1), 84–100. https://doi.org/10.1111/j.1467-9248.1994.tb01675.x.

Wirz, M. & Wernau, J. (2016, 3 April). Tuna and gunships: How $850 million in bonds went bad in Mozambique. *Wall Street Journal.* http://www.wsj.com/articles/tuna-and-gunships-how-850-million-in-bonds-went-bad-in-mozambique-1459675803.

World Bank. (2011). World development indicators. http://data.worldbank.org/indicator/NY.GDP.PCAP.CD. Accessed on 8 September 2011.

Wynter, S. (2001). Towards the sociogenic principle: Fanon, the puzzle of conscious experience, of "identity" and what it's like to be "black." In A. Gomez-Moriana & M. Duran-Cogan (Eds.), *National identities and socio-political changes in Latin America* (1st edition). New York: Routledge.

Zanotti, L. (2011). *Governing disorder: UN Peace operations, international security, and democratization in the post–Cold War era.* Penn State Press.

Zartman, I. W. (Ed.). (1995). *Collapsed states: The disintegration and restoration of legitimate authority.* Lynne Rienner.

Zaum, D. (2007). *The sovereignty paradox: The norms and politics of international statebuilding.* Oxford; New York: Oxford University Press.

Index

Mozambique, overview
  flag design, 85
  historical presence in, 41, 60
  political consciousness engagement
    in, 44, 60
  population demographics, 84
  postcolonial war and destabilisation
    of, 61, 62, 87, 105, 106
  research study descriptions, 9–10
  salaries, national average, 127
  See also related topics
Mozambique National
  Resistance. *See* Renamo
MST. *See Movimento Sem Terra*
Mueda, 124–25
murders, 63, 119

Nabi, Gulam, 117
National AIDS Council, 65
National Plan for Strategic Investment
    in Agriculture. *See* Plano Nacional
    de Investimento no Sector Agrario
National Union of Peasant Farmers. *See*
    União Nacional de Camponeses
Négritude movement, 39, 43, 44
neoliberalism, 5, 32–33, 34, 46, 79, 139
New Man ideology, 61, 118
NGOs (national government
    organisations), 68–69, 73, 88,
    90–91, 113
Nhamirre, Borges, 120
Nhantumbo, Noe, 113, 115–16
Norway, 67, 113
Noticias (newspaper), 115
Nuvunga, Adriano, 113, 114
Nyusi, Filipe, 123

oppression, 23, 52–54
Organização Rural De Ajuda Mútua/
    Organisation for Rural Mutual
    Assistance (ORAM), 100–101
Organisation for Economic
    Co-operation and Development
    (OECD), 63
Orientalism, 20–21

Otherness ontologies, 27–30
ownership, local *vs.* national, 63, 66, 76,
    77, 132

Paffenholz, Thania, 30
Panama Papers, 144
PAPA. *See* Plano de Acção da Produção
    Agricola
Paris, Roland, 19, 34
Paris Declaration on Aid
    Effectiveness, 63, 66, 76, 77,
    132, 144
PARP/PARPA. *See* Plano de Acção para
    Redução da Pobreza Absoluta
patriarchy, 48
Pavignani, Enrico, 68
peacebuilding and peacekeeping
  colonial difference
    acknowledgement, 31, 138–39
  as intervention component, 5, 18
  liberal strategies, 26, 28, 34,
    39, 40–41
  post-liberal strategies, 28–30, 32,
    35, 140
Peaceland (Autesserre), 30–31, 138, 141
Peace Operations Seen from Below
    (Pouligny), 13n7
peasant farmers (*camponeses*), 54,
    84–88, 95, 100–101, 103–8
  See also agricultural development
PEDSA. *See* Plano Estratégico para
    o Desenvolvimento do Sector
    Agrário
PEPFAR. *See* President's Emergency
    Plan for AIDS Relief
per diem payments, 134
perspectival realism, 8, 52
Pfeiffer, James, 68–69, 126–27
pharmaceuticals, 64–65
Plano de Acção da Produção Agricola
    (PAPA), 98
Plano de Acção para Redução da
    Pobreza Absoluta (PARP/PARPA,
    Poverty Reduction Strategy Papers,
    PRSP), 63, 77, 81n2, 86

About the Author

Meera Sabaratnam is Senior Lecturer in International Relations at SOAS, University of London. She is a founding co-convenor of the Colonial / Postcolonial / De-colonial Working Group of the British International Studies Association, founding member of *The Disorder of Things* blog and an Online Editor for *International Studies Quarterly*. She co-edited the volumes *Interrogating Democracy in World Politics* (2011, with Joe Hoover and Laust Schouenborg) and *A Liberal Peace? The Problems and Practices of Peacebuilding* (2011, with Susanna Campbell and David Chandler).

CPSIA information can be obtained
at www.ICGtesting.com
Printed in the USA
LVHW011645190222
711543LV00004B/108